Technological Resources and the Logic of Corporate Diversification

This impressive book sees the author applying and expanding the resource-based view of the firm to explain and predict the strategy of corporate diversification. The book extends the current theory in the following ways:

- using more fine-grained microanalytic analysis;
- exploiting patent data to link a firm's technological diversification to its product diversification opportunities;
- extending links to transaction cost economics;
- analyzing the modes by which corporate diversification occurs.

Technological Resources and the Logic of Corporate Diversification is an original and authoritative book that will be extremely useful to academics and students in such disciplines as business economics, corporate strategy, and international business.

Brian S. Silverman is Associate Professor at the University of Toronto.

Studies in Global Competition

A series of books edited by John Cantwell, University of Reading, UK and David Mowery, University of California, Berkeley, USA

Technological Resources and the Logic of Corporate Diversification

Brian S. Silverman

London and New York

First published 2002 by Routledge
11 New Fetter Lane, London EC4P 4EE

Simultaneously published in the USA and Canada
by Routledge
29 West 35th Street, New York, NY 10001

Routledge is an imprint of the Taylor & Francis Group

© 2002 Brian S. Silverman

Typeset in Goudy by Wearset Ltd, Boldon, Tyne and Wear
Printed and bound in Great Britain by TJ International Ltd, Padstow,
Cornwall

British Library Cataloguing in Publication Data
A catalogue record for this book is available from the British Library

Library of Congress Cataloging in Publication Data
A catalog record for this book has been requested

ISBN 0–415–27136–3

Contents

Figures

Tables

Preface

This study applies and extends the resource-based view of the firm as it pertains to corporate diversification. More specifically, this study endeavors to (1) define and measure technological resources at a more microanalytic level than has been done in prior research, (2) extend and refine the hypotheses concerning diversification derived from the resource-based framework by integrating it with transaction cost economics, and (3) derive and test hypotheses about aspects of diversification other than its direction and the resulting performance – in particular, about the mode by which such diversification occurs.

Previous studies of diversification have used R&D intensity as a proxy for technological resources, and have found that firms with high R&D intensities tend to diversify into industries with high R&D intensities. However, research into firm-specific "technological competence" suggests that a particular technological ability or knowledge is useful in only a narrow range of applications, an effect that is not captured by aggregate R&D statistics. Put another way, the results of prior studies cannot tell us whether a pharmaceutical company is more likely to diversify into biotechnology or electronics. Through the development of a new methodology to link patents to industries in which they are likely to be applicable, this study generates a more precise measure of technological resources than has been constructed previously. This measure supports the testing of more finely grained hypotheses concerning corporate diversification than previous empirical research has enjoyed, and is hypothesized to significantly improve the explanatory power of resource-based models of diversification.

Resource-based theorists have typically implicitly assumed that contracting out excess rent-producing resources is an infeasible alternative to diversification. This study tests the validity of that assumption. Explicit application of transaction cost economics to the resource-based framework suggests that some resources can and will be contracted out. In particular, firms will exploit through contracting those resources that are subject to low degrees of contractual hazards. Diversification – the expansion of a firm's boundaries in order to exploit resources – will be pursued only when contractual hazards are severe.

The role of technological resources and contractual hazards on firms' diversification behavior is the focus of an empirical study. This research draws on several large databases to generate a sample of diversifying entry (and non-entry) by 412 US firms into 429 four-digit SIC businesses between 1981 and 1985. The logit method is used to test a series of hypotheses. Strong support is found for the explanatory power of the new technological resource measures and for the role of contractual hazards in determining whether firms exploit their technological resources by diversification or by contractual means. Technological resources are also found to influence the mode by which diversification is effected.

Acknowledgments

As I write this brief note of thanks to those without whom this study would be incomplete, I fear that I may be accused of boosterism, or, worse yet, provincialism. Nevertheless, I must say that I cannot imagine a better place at which to write a dissertation today than at the University of California at Berkeley. My mentors at the Haas School of Business and in other departments, and even more so my colleagues in the Haas Ph.D. program, have had an impact on my research interests and my way of thinking far beyond my highest pre-Berkeley hopes. As someone on this list might say, consider these *seriatim*:

I am indebted to my dissertation chair, David Teece. His work on technology strategy played a central role in my thinking and in my interest in the subject, without which I likely would not have ever made it to the University of California. His work on capabilities helped broaden my interests to encompass issues of general strategy. His influence can clearly be seen in this study.

My dissertation committee members each devoted more time and effort to this project than I had any right to expect. Each is directly responsible for making this study far better than it otherwise would have been. Each will remain with me as a role model as I work with my own students in the future.

It is difficult to overstate the role played by David Mowery as a mentor on this and other research projects. He has acted as teacher of the first course I took at UC-Berkeley, adviser on my second-year paper, leader of research projects at SEMATECH and at the US national laboratories, challenger and supporter of the research in this study, and co-author on several papers. I am grateful for his efforts in all of these capacities, and feel fortunate to be able to call him an adviser, colleague, and friend.

Oliver Williamson played a major role in my personal "fundamental transformation" from student to academic. The force of his thinking has changed my understanding about economics and organization. His commitment to high standards of research significantly improved this work. (I will not soon forget the real-life lessons in sequentially adaptive bargaining and credible commitments involved in raising this study to his professional standards.) I am grateful for his advice and participation on this project.

Bronwyn Hall also played a major role in my dissertation research. Without her willingness to devote time and insight to this project, this study would have taken twice as long to complete and would have been half as good. In particular, Bronwyn shared her understanding of patent statistics, econometrics, and economic theory to ensure that this project would be well-grounded theoretically and empirically. I am deeply grateful to her for remaining actively involved in this project even when she was 7000 miles away at Oxford and the Sorbonne.

Several other faculty members have offered comments and criticism on portions of this study. In particular, I am grateful to Glenn Carroll, Shane Greenstein, Trond Petersen, Carl Shapiro, and Pablo Spiller for their advice and insight.

Virtually all of the students that have passed through the Haas Business and Public Policy Ph.D. program during the last five years have played some role in improving this study. I express particular appreciation to Janet Bercovitz, Tom Cottrell, John de Figueiredo, Jackson Nickerson, Joanne Oxley, Eric Thacker, and Emerson Tiller for their comments on the ideas presented herein.

I am indebted to Professor Samuel Kortum for generously making available to me the Canadian Patent Office data extract used in this study. In addition to providing this extract, Sam spent considerable time providing documentation and explaining the subtleties of the data.

I am similarly indebted to Professors Carl Voigt and Richard Rumelt for their willingness to make available to me the AGSM/Trinet Large Establishment database. Carl also devoted a great deal of time to ensure that I understood the nuances of this data set. Finally, I am indebted to Professor F.M. Scherer for providing me with data on the 100 patents that he had used in his evaluation of the Office of Technology Assessment and Forecasting's patent concordance. Although he did not know me, Mike Scherer immediately sent to me all of his original documentation regarding these patents after a single phone call during which I introduced myself and explained my interest in the data. His only condition was that I return the data when I was finished. I can only assume that I was uncharacteristically polite and charming during our phone call.

Thanks also to Gwen Cheeseburg, Lee Forgue, Jan Greenough, Pat Murphy, Anita Patterson, Debbie Richerson, and Stephanie Tibbets, each of whom helped me to overcome various administrative hurdles in the Haas Ph.D. program.

I would also like to thank the Bradley Fellowship and the Sloan Foundation for research support during my time at the University of California, the Connaught Foundation and the Social Sciences and Humanities Research Council for research support during my time at University of Toronto, and the Division of Research at Harvard Business School for research support during my years at that institution.

Finally, I thank my wife, Hannah, my daughter, Arkady, and my parents, Myron and Judith, for their support throughout this endeavor.

1   Introduction

Overview

Corporate diversification[1] is a ubiquitous feature of the modern economic land-scape. For most US firms, "[a] long-term continuing strategy of growth [has been based on] expansion into new geographical or product markets" (Chandler 1992: 83). The expansion of corporate boundaries to include new lines of business has occurred not only within large Fortune 500 corporations (Rumelt 1974) but also within many smaller firms (Teece *et al.* 1994).[2] Despite the prevalence of multiproduct corporations, however, until recently there has been little theory with which to explain or predict diversification.

In contrast to this theoretical dearth, there has been a great deal of empirical exploration of corporate diversifying behavior. Scholars have placed particular emphasis on (1) uncovering empirical regularities in diversification activity,[3] (2) exploring the links between diversification and firm performance,[4] and (3) constructing indices with which to measure the extent of a firm's diversifica-tion.[5] However, perhaps because of the lack of theoretical foundations to guide this research, little progress has been made in the empirical literature on diversi-fication since the landmark studies of the 1960s and 1970s (Ramanujam and Varadarajan 1989).

In the last decade, the recently developed resource-based view of the firm (Wernerfelt 1984; Barney 1986; Teece 1988) has been touted as particularly conducive to understanding corporate diversification. This conducivity notwithstanding, the operationalization of this theory has been limited to broad characterization of resources and the industries to which they might fruitfully be applied. For example, studies have found that firms with high R&D intensities tend to diversify into industries with high R&D intensities. But research into firm-specific "technical competence" (e.g., Pavitt *et al.* 1989; Patel and Pavitt 1994; Jaffe 1986) suggests that a particular technological ability or knowledge is useful in only a very narrow range of applications. This suggests that the opera-tionalization of resource-based theory might be usefully informed by the narrowly defined technological capabilities proposed in the technological competence literature.

In this study I apply and extend the resource-based view of the firm to explain and predict corporate diversification. My efforts to extend the theory follow three avenues. First, I define and measure technological resources at a more microanalytic level than has been done in prior resource-based research. This enables me to integrate elements of the technological competence and resource-based literatures to shed further light on firms' diversifying behavior. In particular, I develop a new methodology to link patents to industries in which they are likely to be applicable. Using this methodology, I am able to create a new database that links firms' patent portfolios – which are indicators (albeit noisy) of corporate technological competence (Patel and Pavitt 1994) – to their output in product markets. This database supports the testing of more finely grained hypotheses concerning corporate diversification than previous empirical research has enjoyed.

Second, by stressing the resource-based framework's links to transaction cost economics, I attempt to draw out a more complete set of resource-based hypotheses than has been done in the past. Most prior research in this framework has implicitly or explicitly assumed that the resources that provide value to firms are necessarily too asset-specific to allow contracting. Rather than make this assumption, I explicitly develop and test hypotheses concerning the possibility of contractual alternatives to diversification, finding evidence that firms diversify when alternatives are subject to high contracting hazards.

Third, I extend the reach of the resource-based view by deriving and testing hypotheses about aspects of diversification other than its direction and the resulting performance – in particular, about the mode by which such diversification occurs (acquisition or internal expansion).

This study should add to our knowledge about the role of resources in general, and technological resources in particular, as artifacts upon which a firm may build its downstream product portfolio. Resource-driven corporate diversification is a topic that has both scholarly and practical implications. The development of the resource-based view of the firm has led numerous scholars to prescribe that firms should focus on developing "core competences" from which business- and product-level competitive advantage will naturally flow (see, for example, Prahalad and Hamel 1990). However, the nature of these competences and their methods of exploitation remain somewhat mysterious, and rarely obvious except through *ex post* analysis. An enhanced understanding of how important attributes of technological resources drive a firm's decision to diversify (or to pursue an alternative mechanism of exploitation) would provide insights into the nature of resource-based rents and their variation across firms and industries. This has both normative and positive implications for theories of competitive strategy, theories of the management of innovation, and theories of the firm.

Context of the study

The present study examines diversification behavior in a sample of US manufacturing firms during the first half of the 1980s. The sample includes 344 firms randomly selected from the 573 US firms with the largest number of patent assignments during the 1970s (see Jaffe 1986 for the entire universe of these firms), and 68 firms randomly selected from the population of all other US firms that appear in the major firm-level databases used in this study (Compustat; *Who Owns Whom*; and the AGSM/Trinet Large Establishment database). This study relies heavily on technology-intensive firms because the key resources under consideration are technological resources, as measured by patent portfolios.

A multi-industry sample of US firms offers several benefits for the purposes of the present study. First, numerous studies of corporate diversification have examined similar samples of firms (Montgomery and Wernerfelt 1988; Montgomery and Hariharan 1991). Since this study seeks to improve upon prior research, my conducting research on a sample of firms similar to those used before facilitates the comparison of this study's results with those of its precursors. Second, the focus on multiple industries allows the incorporation of industry-specific variables as well as firm-specific variables to determine how the relationship between technological resources and corporate diversification patterns varies across industries as well as firms. Finally, a practical benefit of such a multi-industry study of US firms is the availability of relatively detailed information about the firms, their activities, and their technological resources. This type of detailed information is essential for a study of this nature. The sources and nature of the data used in this study are discussed below.

Sources of data

The empirical research undertaken in this study relies on several sources of data. The AGSM/Trinet Large Establishment database (Trinet) was compiled for every odd-numbered year between 1979 and 1989.[6] Trinet includes information on corporate ownership, employment, and four-digit SIC code of operations for more than 400,000 establishments in the United States (see Table 1.1).[7] For establishments in which multiple four-digit SIC businesses are undertaken, Trinet provides up to three separate SIC codes (with SIC-specific employee breakdowns).[8]

Information on firms' patent portfolios came from two sources: The Micropatent PatentSearch database and the Canadian Patent Office PATDAT database. The Micropatent PatentSearch database includes every patent granted by the United States Patent and Trademark Office between 1975 and the present. For each patent, this database includes the date on which the patent application was submitted, the firm to which it was assigned (if any), and the technology class to which it was assigned, as well as other information from the first page of the issued patent (see Table 1.2). The PATDAT database

Table 1.1 Information available in the AGSM/Trinet database*

Establishment ID no.
Establishment name
Establishment address
  Street
  City
  County
  State
  Zip code
Establishment business (Four-digit SIC)
Number of employees involved
Estimated sales
Parent ID no.
Parent name
Parent HQ address
  Street
  City
  County
  State
  Zip code

Note
*Fields used in this study are shown in boldface.

Table 1.2 Information available on the front page of US patents* (1)

Patent number
Title
Application date
Grant date
Inventor(s)
State/country of inventor(s)
Assignee
Type of applicant (individual, non-profit, for-profit private, government)
US patent class (USPC)
International patent class (IPC)
US references
Foreign references
References to publications
Abstract
Claims

Note
*Fields used in this study are shown in boldface.

includes every patent issued by the Canadian Patent Office between 1978 and 1993.[9] In addition to providing information on the patent class to which each patent was assigned, it also provides the (Canadian) four-digit SIC industry of use and the (Canadian) four-digit industry of manufacture to which the patent was assigned. Dun and Bradstreet's *Who Owns Whom. North America* (1981) was used to link patent-owning subsidiaries with their parents.

Overall, these databases represent some of the most comprehensive available sources of information on corporate diversification behavior and on corporate technological resources. Nevertheless, additional sources were tapped to extend and complement this information. The "Yale study" of innovation (Levin *et al.* 1987) provides information on the effectiveness of various mechanisms for appropriating returns generated by technological innovation (i.e., licensing of patents, reliance on trade secrets). This information is used as a proxy for the feasibility of a firm's using contractual alternatives to diversification to exploit its technology. The Federal Trade Commission's Line of Business database (US Federal Trade Commission 1975, 1976), the *Census of Manufactures* (1982, 1987), and the *Annual Survey of Manufactures* (1981–1985) all provide information on industry-level variables of interest such as industry concentration, industry growth, and industry average R&D- and advertising-intensity. Finally, the Compustat database (1977–1985) provides information for firm-level variables of interest such as firm size, firm growth, and firm R&D- and advertising-intensity.

Organization of the study

This study is organized as follows. Chapter 2 examines the theoretical and empirical literature relevant to corporate diversification. The review of the various theoretical lenses suggests that there is to date only a partial understanding of the determinants of diversifying behavior. The chapter also briefly describes the technological competence literature, a subset of the resource-based view that – while not directly related to questions of diversification – suggests that existing conceptions of technological resources in the empirical literature on diversification are unsatisfactory, and offers clues as to fruitful ways to improve the operationalization of these technological resources.

Chapter 3 develops a conceptual framework around the theoretical perspectives discussed in Chapter 2: the resource-based view (with a particular emphasis on its transaction cost roots) and the technological competence literature. Several propositions are derived, primarily pertaining to the direction of diversification, the feasibility of contractual alternatives to diversification, and the mode through which diversification is effected.

Chapter 4 reviews several alternate measures of technological resources: R&D statistics, innovation counts, and patent data. After concluding that patents are in general the best available indicators of technological prowess, and that their chief weakness is the inability to connect them to the businesses in which they offer competitive advantage, the chapter introduces a new methodology to link patents to the industries in which they are likely to be useful. The chapter also demonstrates that this newly developed patent-SIC concordance offers a more accurate linkage than the other concordances available previously.

Chapter 5 tests a set of hypotheses concerning the extent to which a firm's existing technological resources contour its subsequent diversification activity. These hypotheses are tested with data on 2514 diversification entries and non-entries between 1981 and 1985. Chapter 6 examines the factors affecting the mode of diversification. A set of hypotheses concerning the decision to diversify via internal growth as opposed to acquisition are derived and tested with data on 1023 diversification entries between 1981 and 1985.

Chapter 7 concludes with a summary of the results of this study and a discussion of their implications for future research.

2 Review of prior theoretical and empirical research on diversification

This chapter is divided into four sections. The first provides an overview of theoretical perspectives that bear on the diversification phenomenon. It highlights the contributions that each of several efficiency-based theories – neoclassical economics (economies of scope), transaction cost economics and the resource-based view – have made to our understanding of corporate diversification. The second section reviews existing empirical studies of this phenomenon, and interprets their findings through these theoretical lenses. The third section introduces a related literature concerning technological competence. In the fourth section I suggest that the resource-based view and the technological competence literature offer potential for integration that has not yet been fulfilled. I argue that existing empirical tests of resource-based hypotheses concerning diversification, by not focusing sufficiently on the attributes of resources (as the technological competence literature does), have left a gap in the literature. This gap is the subject of the next chapter.

Theoretical research: efficiency theories of diversification[1]

Neoclassical economics

In the neoclassical economics framework, the firm is conceived to be a production function. Resting on strict assumptions of rationality and generally free-flowing (or inexpensively accessed) information, the neoclassical view posits a world in which all production technologies exist as well-defined blueprints; economic actors can select their desired production technology from this set of blueprints. Given this emphasis on well-defined productive capacities, with firm-specific knowledge and differential organizational or managerial abilities assumed away, it is not surprising that neoclassical theory predicts product diversification solely on the basis of idiosyncrasies in particular production technologies. Specifically, a firm engaged in the production of product X will diversify into production of product Y if and only if its production technology is such that the total cost of jointly producing X and Y is less than the total cost of producing X and Y separately – that is, when $C(X,Y) < C(X,0) + C(0,Y)$. This cost structure is defined as economies of scope (Panzar and Willig 1975; Baumol et al. 1982).

Transaction cost economics

Transaction cost economics proposes that economic actors "align transactions (which differ in their attributes) with governance structures (costs and competencies of which differ) in a discriminating (mainly, transaction cost economizing) way" (Williamson 1988: 73). Resting on the behavioral assumptions of bounded rationality and opportunism, transaction cost economics asserts that, contingent on the environmental factors of uncertainty and thickness of markets, transactions will be located in governance structures based on their characteristics – chiefly complexity, frequency, and asset-specificity (Williamson 1975, 1985; Klein *et al.* 1978). The theory thus offers a framework involving comparative institutional analysis to infer which mode of organization – market, hierarchy, or hybrid – will best govern a given transaction (Williamson 1991).

Transaction cost economists thus view the firm in terms of both production and organization technologies. By focusing on the potential of and limitations to contractual agreements, the transaction cost approach suggests that economies of scope in production are neither necessary nor sufficient to generate multiproduct firms. Scope economies are not sufficient because, barring transaction cost problems such as thin markets, the producer of X whose production technology offers such economies for the production of Y can contract out the Y-producing services of its factors. Production scope economies are not necessary because, in the face of "tacit" knowledge (knowledge that is difficult or impossible to transfer) developed in the process of using some production technology, even without economies of scope the firm must rely on internal production to use its knowledge fully. Rather, it is the existence of high transaction costs generated by asset-specificity and the tacit nature of certain assets (such as know-how) that lead to the integration of multiple products within one firm (Teece 1982).

The transaction cost lens has been used primarily to examine the make-or-buy decision – that is, to explain the firm's decision to diversify into vertically related industries (more commonly referred to as vertical integration). Nevertheless, the transaction cost framework offers prescriptions for horizontal diversification that resemble those for vertical integration: contract out the excess services of corporate assets unless the nature of the transaction is such that in-house exploitation of the excess services is less costly (Teece 1980, 1982). This prescription provides an idea of the circumstances under which the services of assets will be contracted out as opposed to being exploited through expansion of the boundaries of the firm, but it offers little insight in determining the circumstances under which excess resources are likely to be created.

Resource-based framework

During the last decade, scholars have developed a resource-based framework for analyzing business strategy. This framework (which is consonant with research under the names "core competence," "capabilities," etc.) draws heavily on both transaction cost economics and evolutionary economic theory, particularly as propounded by Penrose. Contemporary evolutionary economics focuses on the organization as the economic analogue of a biological organism; the organization's roles, policies, and routines serve as its genetic code (Alchian 1950; Nelson and Winter 1982). Much as in biological evolution, organizations compete to survive in a selection environment whose strictness can vary. Organizations that embody superior (i.e., more efficient, more flexible in the face of adaptive pressure) routines will grow, while those burdened with less advantageous routines will be, to put it euphemistically, "selected out."

Although Nelson and Winter are the scholars most closely associated with evolutionary economics today, it was their predecessor Edith Penrose who authored the literature's most direct treatment of corporate diversification.[2] In her *Theory of the Growth of the Firm* (1959), Penrose adopts Schumpeter's ([1942] 1950) view that, traditional economic theory notwithstanding, chronic disequilibrium is far more prevalent in a capitalist economy than is long-term equilibrium. One manifestation of this chronic disequilibrium is that a firm generates disequilibrium pressures to expand simply in the course of pursuing its regular operations – essentially, as a firm continually becomes more efficient at its operations by virtue of its accumulation of operating experience, it continually creates excess resources (such as spare time) with which to grow.[3] Penrose suggests that these excess resources will be channeled into growth in the firm's extant product markets until such growth is constrained by limits to market demand. A firm will prefer to deploy excess resources in existing markets rather than into new markets because the former is less costly than the latter. A firm's managers are already familiar with their current businesses; consequently, they need to expend fewer resources (i.e., less managerial time) to manage continued deployment in these markets than in new markets. When the firm generates excess resources at a faster rate than it can redeploy them in its primary market, it will diversify. Specifically, a firm will diversify into those industries in which the firm's excess resources will offer the greatest advantage.

Drawing largely on the Penrosian framework, the resource-based framework suggests that the firm is best viewed as a collection of sticky and difficult-to-imitate resources and capabilities that enable it to compete against other firms successfully (Wernerfelt 1984; Barney 1986; Teece *et al.* 1994). These resources can be either physical, such as production techniques protected by patents or trade secrets, or intangible, such as brand equity or operating routines. Of particular importance is the specificity inherent in such resources: the same characteristics that enable a firm to extract a sustainable rent stream from these assets often make it nearly impossible for the firm to "transplant" them and utilize them effectively in a new context. Thus, a firm that has developed an advantageous resource position is protected to the extent that its resources are specific; at the same time, this specificity constrains the firm's ability to transfer these resources to new uses (Montgomery and Wernerfelt 1988). The resource-based framework has thus far yielded three general hypotheses concerning diversification: (1) firms should (or will) diversify into businesses in which they can exploit their resources, (2) firms with highly specific resources should (or will) diversify more narrowly, and (3) firms that behave according to the first two hypotheses will enjoy superior performance to those that do not.

It should be noted that the Penrosian framework is usefully informed by transaction cost reasoning. Penrose cites three categories of likely excess resources: indivisibilities in productive resources, the freeing up of productive resources due to increased specialization (or learning curve effects), and the freeing up of managerial resources.[4] Her framework implicitly assumes that exploitation of excess resources necessitates their use within the firm. As a logical consequence of this assumption, Penrose's framework is unidirectional – firms grow but never shrink; firms acquire but never divest. However, the transaction cost perspective asks whether there are alternative ways to utilize these assets, including outside contracting and spin-offs (Teece 1980). Transaction cost economics also offers a rationale for the potential benefits of contracting out excess resources (incentive intensity) and suggests circumstances in which excess resources will be better spun off from the company.[5] This suggests that a more complex focus on the attributes of excess resources is necessary to determine their effect on corporate diversification.

Resource-based theorists have generally acknowledged the insight of transaction cost economics, but have neither tested nor fully assimilated its implications. Montgomery and Hariharan (1991) explicitly assume that the resources they investigate – technological and marketing skills – are difficult to transfer, and Montgomery (1994) contends that resources to which rent accrues are likely to be specific and therefore difficult to contract out. However, Chatterjee and Wernerfelt (1991) include financial reserves in their typology of resources as a resource likely to fuel successful unrelated diversification. A transaction cost approach would suggest that such a fungible resource has no place on a list of resources that drive successful diversification.[6]

Within the resource-based field, there is a debate over the temporal nature of resources and rent. Some theorists have emphasized the firm's use of its given set of resources rather than the process through which such resources are acquired or created.[7] Others, focusing on what they call "capabilities," have stressed the "flow" nature of resources.[8] Of particular importance to these theorists are the cumulative processes by which such unique resources are created and dissipated (Dierickx and Cool 1989; Pavitt *et al.* 1989; Teece *et al.* 1992). The capabilities branch thus tends to rely more heavily on evolutionary theory than does the resource-based view because of its greater emphasis on routines and path-dependence as mechanisms by which firms can renew, alter, or dissipate their resource positions. In large part, this debate boils down to differing views on the sustainability of rents – if a given resource will generate a sustainable rent stream for a long period of time, then analysis of resource stocks is sufficient to inform corporate strategy and performance. If the resource's rent stream is not sustainable, then one must focus on the forces that affect resource flows. This theoretical debate is of considerable interest, but it cannot be settled without recourse to longitudinal empirical analysis, which can inform the fundamental issue of rent sustainability. To the best of my knowledge, no such research has yet been performed.[9]

Empirical studies of diversification

Empirical research relevant to resource-based hypotheses of diversification can generally be divided into two categories: studies that track firms' propensities to diversify in certain broad directions, and studies that attempt to attribute different performance results to different resource position–diversification strategy combinations.

Propensity for certain firms to diversify in certain directions

In the first major study of corporate diversification in the United States, Gort (1962) used three-digit SIC data to develop measures of diversification for several hundred US firms. Gort found that (1) diversification is negatively related to the market growth rate of a firm's primary industry, (2) diversification is positively related to R&D intensity,[10] and (3) firms tend to diversify into businesses that are similar to their existing businesses in terms of R&D intensity and advertising intensity. While Gort did not establish causality, his results may be interpreted to suggest that firms tend to redeploy their resources into their existing businesses until such redeployment is constrained by market demand, and that diversifying firms can exploit strong technological skills in businesses requiring technological skills. In addition, the higher incidence of diversification for R&D-intensive firms suggests that R&D activity creates transferable (presumably technology-based) sources of competitive advantage. These results are broadly consistent with the implications of resource-based theory, in that difficult-to-imitate or difficult-to-transfer resources and skills appear to be at the center of the firm's decision to diversify.

Subsequent empirical studies have generally corroborated Gort's research.[11] Chandler (1977, 1990) concluded from his analysis of US, UK and German companies' histories that diversification was a "rational response" by managers whose firms enjoyed high levels of technological or administrative ability. Teece (1980) found that petroleum firms tended to diversify into those alternative energy sources (and specifically into those functions) in which they could exploit existing strengths. For example, an oil company with experience in shale mining would be likely to diversify into coal mining.[12] Lemelin (1982) used industry-level data to find that firms tend to diversify into industries that have similar levels of R&D and advertising intensities (measured as expenditures divided by sales) to those of the industries in which they already participate. Similarly, Montgomery and Hariharan (1991) used firm-level data from the Federal Trade Commission's Line of Business database to find that firms tend to diversify into industries that have R&D intensities, advertising intensities, and capital expenditure intensities similar to those of the firms' existing businesses.

Diversification strategy and firm performance

In his doctoral dissertation, Rumelt (1974) related corporate diversification to economic performance for a sample of Fortune 500 firms during the 1949–1969 time period. Refining a classification scheme developed by Wrigley (1970), Rumelt classified diversification into seven strategies: single business, dominant-constrained, dominant-vertical, related-constrained, related-linked, unrelated, and conglomerate.[13] He found that firms that pursued a strategy of related diversification – defined as diversification into businesses that shared some "technological or market commonality" with existing businesses – enjoyed systematically higher profitability than those that followed other diversification strategies. Subsequent researchers have proposed competing or complementary explanations for the diversification–performance link as well as alternate measures of diversification and relatedness (i.e., Christensen and Montgomery 1981; Bettis 1981; Rumelt 1982; Baysinger and Hoskisson 1989), but the general findings are broadly consistent with the resource-based contention that firms whose diversification exploits rent-producing assets will enjoy higher performance than firms whose diversification does not.

An alternative approach to testing the performance consequences of diversification has been the study of acquisition announcement events. Several researchers have attempted to categorize diversifying acquisitions by publicly traded corporations as "related" or "unrelated" to test whether the stock market reacts more favorably to announcements of the former type (Singh and Montgomery 1987; Lubatkin 1987; Shleifer and Vishny 1991).[14] These studies have found mixed support at best for resource-based hypotheses; several of these studies find no statistically significant difference in capital market response between related and unrelated acquisitions.

A primary concern regarding this body of empirical work is the method used to identify the degree of relatedness of diversification. Many of these studies have relied on characteristics of the output of industries, and in particular on proximity within the SIC system, to measure relatedness. Three of the most frequently used indices for measuring industry relatedness – the concentric index (Caves *et al.* 1980), the entropy index (Jacquemin and Berry 1979), and the herfindahl (Berry 1974; Palepu 1985) – use proximity within the SIC system to proxy for relatedness. These measures implicitly assume that product similarity is highly correlated with similarity in resource requirements; further, they rely on extremely stringent assumptions about the ordering of the SIC system (for critiques and tests of these measures, see Gollop and Monahan 1991; Davis and Duhaime 1992; Lubatkin *et al.* 1993).

In contrast, three recent studies have focused explicitly on the similarity of industries' resource requirements to determine relatedness. Farjoun (1994) operationalizes industry relatedness by measuring the degree to which two industries use the same types and proportions of human expertise. Using census data at the three-digit SIC level on the extent to which different types of skilled personnel are employed (e.g., chemical engineers, electrical engineers), he finds that a firm will tend to diversify into industries that rely on patterns of such expertise similar to those required in its extant industries. Coff and Hatfield (1995) use similar data in a study of acquisition announcements. They find evidence of significantly higher returns for acquisitions involving firms that are more related in terms of expertise than for firms that are less related along this dimension. Interestingly, they find that a conventional product-based measure of relatedness (the concentric index) yields no difference in returns for their sample. Robins and Wiersema (1995) operationalize industry relatedness as the degree to which two industries rely on the same inflows of technology. Using Scherer's technology inflow–outflow matrix (a two-digit SIC level analysis), they find that overall corporate performance is significantly higher for firms that have diversified into technologically related industries (in other words, those that draw heavily from the same industries) than for those that have diversified in a more technologically unrelated fashion. Given their emphasis on resource exploitation, these studies appear to be more firmly anchored in the theory than much previous research.

Choice between diversification modes

As Mahoney and Pandian (1992) have pointed out, the resource-based framework (as well as the other above-described theories) has been largely silent with respect to the mode of diversification selected by a diversifying firm. Many scholars appear to agree with Ansoff's (1965) proposition that related diversification is likely to be carried out via internal growth while unrelated diversification is more likely to be pursued through acquisition. However, few scholars have attempted to expand upon this contention. Aside from Teece (1982: 58), who suggested that additional factors influencing the mode of diversification include "the nature of the complementary resources [that the firm needs to access]" and the time period over which the firm generates excess resources, most scholars have focused on developing rationales to support Ansoff's relatedness–internal growth prescription.

Given the influence of Ansoff's argument, it is worth digressing for a moment to consider it. Ansoff (1965) proposed that firms diversify to pursue "synergy," broadly defined as any situation in which costs can be spread over additional activities.[15] Ansoff went on to decompose synergy into "startup" and "operating" synergy; the former described the firm's ability to mitigate the tangible and intangible costs of entering a new business, and the latter described the firm's ability to reduce costs once the new business was a going concern. Ansoff argued that a firm would choose its direction of diversification based on both startup and operating synergy. However, in his discussion of the "make or buy" decision facing the diversifying firm, Ansoff (1965: 196–200) focused primarily on the startup phase, to the exclusion of implications for ongoing operations: "Two primary variables influences the choice between the major [mode] alternatives. These are the startup cost and the timing." Subsequent researchers have tended to perpetuate this underemphasis on post-startup issues by explaining the related–internal choice motivation as driven by features of startup costs, capital market imperfections that affect a firm's ability to finance acquisitions, and barriers to entry.

Considering the lack of theory concerning the mode of diversification, it is not surprising that empirical research has largely ignored the diversifying firm's modal decision. Several studies of diversification have focused exclusively on one mode, be it acquisition (Salter and Weinhold 1979; Ansoff *et al.* 1971; all of the above-mentioned studies of abnormal capital market returns) or internal growth (Biggadike 1979). To date, only three empirical studies have investigated the modal choice of diversifying firms.[16]

In his doctoral dissertation, Yip (1982) developed and tested a model that explained choice of diversification mode as a function of (1) barriers to entry and (2) relatedness of diversification.[17] Using PIMS data for 59 diversifying entries during the 1970s, Yip found no direct evidence to support his contention (*à la* Ansoff) that firms rely on internal growth when they diversify into related industries and acquisitions otherwise. While Yip interpreted his results to offer indirect support for the role of relatedness, the fact remains that neither of his relatedness variables is statistically significant. In particular, neither a subjective variable categorizing the diversification entry as related or unrelated nor a survey-based variable measuring the extent to which activities could be "shared" between the entered business and extant businesses was significant.[18]

Chatterjee (1990), in what may be the only explicitly resource-based analysis of this issue, examined 144 diversification entries by 47 Fortune 500 firms in the early 1960s. Chatterjee argued that while acquisition can be used by a firm to acquire needed resources, it was also likely to burden the firm with unneeded or redundant resources that could not easily be sold piecemeal. He hypothesized that related acquisition was more likely than unrelated acquisition to saddle the firm with such redundant assets, and consequently that firms pursuing related diversification would use internal expansion.[19] As did Yip, he found no statistically significant support for his hypothesis that the relatedness of diversification influences modal choice.[20] Finally, Amit *et al.* (1989), in an attempt to test various hypotheses concerning diversification mode choice, ignored issues of relatedness entirely.[21]

Technological competence

As should be evident from the previous section, theoretical analysis in the resource-based view has stressed highly application-specific, narrowly transferable resources. Empirical research in this area, however, has generally contented itself with aggregate resource measures, such as R&D intensity to proxy for technological resources. A related stream of literature, focusing on technological competence, has spawned measures of technology that are more finely grained, and that are arguably more appropriate for empirical analysis of resource-based hypotheses.

The literature on technological competence largely resembles, and is often considered a subset of, the resource-based framework. Technological competence refers to an organization's ability to develop and design products and processes (Dosi and Teece 1993).[22] In addition to providing relative technological advantage *vis-à-vis* other firms, technological competence also strongly influences the direction of future technological search activities. Further, there is (or should be) a strong link between a firm's technological competence and its downstream activities such as product range (Patel and Pavitt 1994).

The technological competence literature differs from the larger set of resource-based literature primarily in the operationalization of such technological capability. Rather than look at aggregate R&D resources, several scholars in the technological competence branch have examined individual innovations or patents (or portfolios of patents) to identify at a more disaggregated level the elements that comprise technological capability. Such work has led to insights that are obscured by reliance on R&D data.

For example, an in-depth study of several thousand innovations throughout the British economy since the Second World War found that firms' directions of innovative capability were largely stable over a 40-year period (Pavitt *et al.* 1989). Similarly, studies of corporate patent portfolios in the US suggest that firms have been able to alter the direction of their technological strengths only gradually (Jaffe 1986, 1989a).[23] Finally, several studies have used the technological area in which a firm's patents are classified to proxy for the specific technological areas in which a firm is particularly skilled (Patel and Pavitt 1991, 1994). These studies have demonstrated a strong correlation between the primary business in which a firm competes and the technological areas in which it patents.

The technological competence literature's alternative operationalizations of technological resources have thus allowed insights that otherwise would have eluded resource-based scholars. However, the technological competence literature has failed to address issues surrounding corporate diversification. This is due to the fact that while these studies offer a better measure of technological resources than R&D expenditure, these technology-based measures have thus far not been adequately linked to specific businesses to which they are likely to apply.[24] Without the ability to link patents or innovations to their respective business applications, this literature has remained silent on the question: "How does the firm-specific accumulation of technology interact with opportunities for output diversification (Pavitt 1994: 11)?"

Conclusion

In sum, the resource-based framework has yielded testable hypotheses concerning diversification, and the populous and varied empirical literature on diversification offers moderate support for at least some of these theoretical implications. However, this literature has not yet lived up to the accolades of its supporters. At least three drawbacks have hampered the intellectual growth of the resource-based view of diversification.

First, resource-based theorists have generally neglected to identify and measure resources in a sufficiently discriminating manner to exploit the implications of the framework fully. For all the sophistication of recent empirical research, resource-based scholars have done little more than reconfirm Gort's 30-year-old results. More detailed measurement of a resource's characteristics can significantly proscribe the range of industries in which it can be usefully employed, thus improving the predictive and explanatory power of resource-based hypotheses. For example, as described above, many studies (e.g., Montgomery and Hariharan 1991) have used R&D intensity as a proxy for technological resources and found that firms with high R&D intensities tend to diversify into industries with high R&D intensities. However, this result cannot tell us whether a pharmaceutical company is more likely to diversify into the biotechnology or the computer industry – both of which are R&D-intensive industries. A more detailed characterization of the types of technological knowledge residing in the firm, rather than its aggregate level of expenditure on research, should enable scholars to make more finely grained predictions about the direction of diversification.[25]

Second, transaction cost reasoning suggests that alternative routes for exploiting resources must be explicitly compared to diversification. A more detailed consideration of resource attributes can facilitate the integration of this lens with the resource-based view.

Third, the range of theoretical implications derived from the resource-based framework for diversification has not been fully explored. Virtually all research to date has focused on the framework's implications for the direction of diversification.[26] While an extremely important aspect of corporate diversification, direction is only one dimension of the phenomenon. Others, including the mode of diversification and the phenomenon of divestment, should also be usefully informed by this theory (as is pointed out by Mahoney and Pandian 1992).

3 The effect of resource attributes on the direction, mode, and performance of corporate diversification

Introduction

In this chapter, a conceptual framework is presented for understanding the key resource attributes that affect patterns of diversification. It represents an attempt to incorporate specific attributes of resources into the more generalized resource-based framework.

Direction of diversification

To motivate this framework, let us focus on a firm that has excess or underutilized resources that cannot be deployed in its existing business or businesses (which would be the firm's first choice of deployment, according to Penrose and most subsequent resource-based scholars). Thus, the decision facing the firm is how best to exploit these resources outside of its current operations.

The framework argues that a firm's diversification behavior is a function of three sets of factors. One is the specific range of applications to which the firm's existing resources may be applied. These determine the feasible set of businesses in which the firm's resource base will provide competitive advantage. The second is the extent of transaction costs in the relevant market(s) for the firm's existing resources. These determine the firm's ability to exploit its resources through contractual arrangements, which can obviate the need for expansion of the firm's boundaries. The third set of factors deal with the sustainability of the competitive advantage provided by the firm's resources. It is assumed that a firm cannot act to exploit fully all of its resource potential at once. Given the need for prioritization, a firm will choose to focus first on the exploitation of those resources that offer the most sustainable competitive position. These three sets of factors are considered below.

Range of application

As discussed in Chapter 2, the resource-based theory rests on two fundamental tenets: (1) the fundamental source of competitive advantage for a firm resides in the pool of rent-generating resources that it possesses, (2) these rent-generating resources are useful in a limited range of applications.[1] As a result, a firm whose pool of such resources is underutilized in its current businesses will attempt to exploit them in other businesses, and particularly in one of the businesses in which the resource will generate rents. Integration is one mechanism by which a firm can exploit its resource pool in a new business. Thus, one would expect to find that the target industries into which a firm diversifies are those in which it can exploit its resource pool.

However, precisely because the source of competitive advantage lies in upstream resources and not in downstream product markets (Teece 1982), the range of application of a firm's resource pool is not likely to be discernible by analysis of relatedness among products. Firms that look for product-based similarities rather than resource- or competence-based relatedness are likely to suffer in the marketplace (Prahalad and Hamel 1990). Similarly, scholars who use product-market measures of relatedness are likely to misspecify the true range of application of resources (Coff and Hatfield 1995; Montgomery 1994).

Given the extremely limited range of application attributed to resources (Montgomery and Wernerfelt 1988), use of broad measures such as R&D expenditure or advertising expenditure to proxy for technological and marketing resources is also likely to misspecify the underlying range of application of a firm's resources. Technological competence has an extremely narrow range of applicability that is not captured in R&D statistics (Patel and Pavitt 1994; Teece *et al.* 1994). While less research has been conducted to determine the transferability of marketing resources, it is likely that these too exhibit some narrowness that is not captured in advertising intensity statistics. Similarly, production-related resources, such as specialized manufacturing equipment or experience curve advantages, also face severe obstacles to their transfer to other applications; these restrictions are not captured by use of capital investment intensities.

Thus,

Proposition 1: A firm i that possesses excess or underutilized resources that cannot be employed in its current business(es) is more likely to diversify into business j the more highly applicable its existing resources are to business j, ceteris paribus.

Efficacy of contractual alternatives

What characteristics of resources may influence the level of transaction costs in their exploitation by contractual means? Given their nature, most rent-producing resources involve a significant degree of stickiness (Wernerfelt 1984). For these resources to generate supra-competitive rents they must be in some way difficult to copy, either due to tacit knowledge embedded within them (Polanyi 1958; Teece 1988; Nelson and Winter 1982), to uncertain imitability and causal ambiguity (Lippman and Rumelt 1982; Dierickx and Cool 1989), or to some other failure in resource markets (Barney 1986, 1991). These very characteristics are also likely to create difficulties for a resource-endowed firm that wishes to exploit its resources through the market. While tacitness, uncertainty, or causal ambiguity serve to make resources valuable in the first place, these characteristics also create obstacles for a firm that wishes to exploit its resources through the market. Uncertainty can create problems of moral hazard for contracts (Williamson 1975). In addition, where resources are entangled in tacit knowledge or are otherwise embedded in the firm, even good-faith efforts to transfer resources can founder due to an inability to convey non-codified information (Teece 1977, 1981). To the extent that such hazards arise, transaction cost considerations may require that exploitation of resources be effected through expansion of the firm's boundaries.

Different resources vary in the extent to which they may be efficiently contracted out. There is a large body of literature that suggests that technological resources are likely to face particularly high market failure risks (see for example Pisano 1990; Teece 1977, 1986). Technological resources frequently rest on tacit knowledge; there is quite often a great deal of uncertainty surrounding the potential value of technology and the steps required to achieve this potential (Teece 1982, 1986). Further, market contracts for technological resources can frequently require investments in durable co-specialized assets, which are then vulnerable to hold-up problems (Pisano 1988).[2] Given these features, technological resources are likely to be subject to considerable contractual hazards. Indeed, technological knowledge has been cited as the prototypical non-contractible asset (Teece 1981, 1980; Argyres 1995).

Even within the spectrum of technological resources, however, there is wide variation in the extent of contractual hazards. Numerous sources of data, from the academic-oriented CATI database on joint ventures and strategic alliances (Hagedoorn and Duysters 1993) to the trade journal *Licensing and Economic Review*, list hundreds of technology licensing (hence contractual) agreements between or among firms, providing prima facie evidence that at least in some cases these resources can be efficiently contracted out. In a study of technological innovation in the biotechnology industry during the 1970s and 1980s, Pisano (1990) found that a large number of research projects were undertaken via joint venture – a hybrid arrangement that did not require firms to expand their boundaries as occurs in traditional diversification – and that such arrangements could be explained by transaction cost-related variables surrounding the technology, firms and industry structure involved. Perhaps most interesting, the Yale survey of innovation (Levin *et al.* 1987) uncovered inter-industry variation in the effectiveness of contractual mechanisms for appropriating returns to technological resources.

To the extent that differences exist across technologies (or across the industries in which they are applicable) in the relative efficiency of contracting out technological resources, firms attempting to exploit different technologies should exhibit different patterns of diversification. In particular, transaction cost reasoning suggests that a firm that can efficiently contract out its technological resources into new uses will do so. Diversification will be pursued only if such contracting is subject to sufficiently high hazards to warrant market failure.[3]

Let us return to the motivating example of this chapter: the firm with excess or underutilized resources that it cannot employ in its existing businesses. Such a firm will seek to exploit its resources in new businesses. The governance structure used to effect this exploitation – diversification, contracting out, or some intermediate mechanism – will be determined by the extent to which the resource exploitation is subjected to contractual hazards.

Proposition 2: A firm i that possesses excess or underutilized resources that cannot be employed in its current business(es) is more likely to exploit its resources in new business j through diversification (rather than through contracting out) the more that contracting out its resources to business j is subject to high transaction costs, ceteris paribus.

Sustainability of rent generation by resources

At a given point in time, a firm may find itself with a range of underutilized resources. While different combinations of these resources might support multiple exploitation opportunities, the firm is likely to be constrained regarding the extent to which it can exploit its resources in any given time period. These constraints stem from limitations in managerial time (Penrose 1959). They may also stem from limitations in the firm's ability to finance such exploitation (Teece 1986). Thus, a firm is likely to need to prioritize its resource exploitation. Let us assume that the firm's managers are (boundedly) rational profit-maximizers.[4] Then these managers, faced with need to prioritize their resource exploitation, will make their decisions based on the present value of the expected rents available from various resource combinations. These expected rents are a function of (1) the magnitude of the rents accruing to these resources (which differ by business in which they are exploited, and consequently are a function of the range of resource applicability), and (2) the expected duration of the rent stream, which is a function of the sustainability of the competitive advantage afforded by these resources. The more likely that the firm can sustain its resource-based advantage, the longer that a resource's rent stream will continue into the future, and the larger the present value of this rent.[5]

Proposition 3: A firm i that possesses excess or underutilized resources that cannot be employed in its current business(es) is more likely to diversify into business j the more the rents generated by its resources in business j are sustainable, ceteris paribus.

Mode of diversification

A diversifying firm is likely to find that it does not possess all of the resources required to compete in its new business. The firm has (at least) two options to pursue. The framework suggests that a firm's diversification mode choice is a function of two sets of factors. The first concerns the cost and speed with which a firm can assemble internally the resources required to operate in the entered business. It is argued that internal expansion is favored when resources can be cheaply and quickly built (relative to acquisition).[6] The second concerns the extent to which ongoing operations in the new business must be integrated into, or coordinated with, existing operations. It is argued that internal expansion is favored when a high degree of integration or coordination between the new business and existing operations of the firm is required. It is further argued that both the cost and speed of building and the degree of integration required are largely determined by resource attributes – specifically, by the extent of applicability of the firm's existing resource base to the entered business and by the rate at which "slack" resources are created within the firm.

Building necessary resources: relative cost and speed

Given semi-strong efficient capital markets, a *de novo* entrant should on average incur the same cost to build a business as it would to acquire an existing business of equal size.[7] While acquisitions typically include a premium above the cost of assembling comparable assets (Ansoff 1965), this premium is paid in return for the reduction of startup time and of business risk associated with building a business from scratch. However, this may not hold true for an existing firm that diversifies into a new business. An existing firm that already possesses some of the resources required for the new business may find it cheaper to build rather than buy.

There are two reasons for this. First, it may be the case that a diversifying firm's existing resource base (including managerial knowledge) is at least partially applicable to the new business. To the extent that a firm already has many of the resources required to enter a new business, the time required to build complementary resources is reduced. To the extent that a firm already possesses relevant managerial experience, the expected cost due to early managerial errors is reduced (Ansoff 1965). In these cases, the firm can diversify through internal expansion at a lower-than-average cost and time expenditure. This reduced cost of startup makes internal expansion more attractive relative to acquisition.[8] Second, an acquiree typically includes resources beyond those specifically required for the acquiring firm's diversifying entry. To the extent that these resources duplicate what the acquirer already has, they are redundant or "slack" resources (Chatterjee 1990). Unless these resources enjoy perfect divisibility (Penrose 1959) or contracting free of transaction costs (Williamson 1985), the acquirer is not likely to be able to recoup full value for these resources on the market. To the extent that an acquisition entails purchase of redundant assets that cannot be easily spun off, acquisition is likely to cost more than building comparable resources.

Thus, the range of applicability of a firm's existing resource base has a significant effect on the relative startup cost of internal expansion and acquisition. The more a firm's existing resources are applicable to a new business, the more likely that internal expansion can be effected at lower than average cost and time, and the more likely that acquisition will entail the purchase of redundant resources.

Degree of integration required

To what degree must a diversifying firm integrate a newly entered business into existing operations? Hill *et al.* (1992) argue that firms that pursue related diversification must invest in high levels of interdivisional coordination to exploit the underlying resources properly. According to these scholars, the advantages of related diversification stem from the ability to realize economies of scope across divisions. Effective realization of such scope economies requires interdivisional integration and centralization of decisions regarding the resources from which these scope economies are derived to avoid subgoal pursuit.[9] In contrast, unrelated diversifiers need little interdivisional coordination.[10] Similarly, Argyres (1995) contends that firms must impose greater interdivisional cooperation than the traditional M-form structure prescribes in order to exploit technological core competencies (Prahalad and Hamel 1990).

These arguments are consistent with Mintzberg's (1983) contention that different structures and control systems are needed to implement related and unrelated diversification strategies. Thus, if a firm enters a new business in which its existing resources are applicable, then coordination of these resources across new and existing businesses is of increased importance.[11]

Integration of a new business into existing operations is frequently difficult and costly. More important, integration of acquisitions is typically more difficult to achieve than integration of internal expansions. Acquired firms typically possess their own culture, systems, and routines (Ravenscraft and Scherer 1987). There is a wealth of academic and trade press evidence chronicling the tribulations associated with attempts to assimilate acquired companies. For example, in a survey of large US acquiring firms, Ansoff *et al.* (1971) found that (1) post-acquisition integration problems were experienced by 41 percent of their sample firms, and (2) integration problems increased the greater degree of integration attempted. In contrast, diversification by internal expansion provides for the inculcation of culture, systems, and routines consonant with those of the diversifying firm's existing operations (Hennart and Park 1993).[12] As a result, it is to be expected that diversification that relies on high applicability of a firm's existing resources, which consequently must be more highly integrated with the firm's ongoing operations, will be pursued through internal expansion.

This line of reasoning can draw support from Hill *et al.* (1992), who test empirically the effect on firm performance of the interaction between organizational structure and diversification strategy. Drawing on survey responses about organizational structure from 184 CEOs of Fortune 1000 firms and on diversification and performance data drawn from Compustat, Hill *et al.* find that firms that (1) have pursued related diversification and (2) exhibit a high degree of interdivisional integration and centralization enjoy higher performance than

Table 3.1 Effect of resources on mode of diversification

	Degree to which existing resources are applicable to new business	
	Resources highly applicable to new business	Resources not applicable to new business
Internal expansion	Low cost of building needed resources +	Moderate/high cost of building needed resources 0/–
	High degree of integration required +	Low degree of integration required 0
Acquisition	Moderate cost of acquiring needed resources 0	Moderate cost of acquiring needed resources 0
	High degree of integration required –	Low degree of integration required 0

related diversifiers with lower degrees of integration/centralization. Conversely, firms that (1) have pursued unrelated diversification and (2) exhibit a low degree of interdivisional integration and centralization enjoy higher performance than unrelated diversifiers with higher degrees of integration/centralization.[13]

Table 3.1 summarizes the effects of resource applicability on startup costs and integration costs for internal expansion and for acquisition. It is worth noting that the costs described in this table are extremely difficult to measure. If no steps were taken to make this framework empirically tractable, then the framework would be vulnerable to a charge of tautology. However, while one cannot easily measure startup and integration costs, one can identify attributes of diversifying entries and predict the effect of these attributes on these costs. In particular, this chapter has argued that the cost (and speed) of internal expansion and acquisition is differentially affected by the degree to which the firm's existing resources are applicable to the entered business. The more applicable these resources are, the lower the cost (and higher the speed) of internal expansion relative to acquisition. Further, this chapter has also argued that the cost and difficulty of integrating new operations into existing operations are higher for acquisitions than for internal expansions. Since the degree of resource applicability positively influences the degree to which new businesses must be integrated into existing operations, internal expansion into businesses in which the firm's existing resource pool is highly applicable (and which consequently must be more heavily integrated into existing operations) will incur lower integration costs than acquisition. Diversification into businesses in which the firm's existing resource pool is highly applicable are thus likely to be pursued via internal expansion.[14]

Proposition 4: If a firm i possesses excess or underutilized resources that are highly applicable to industry j and if firm i diversifies into industry j, then firm i will diversify by internal expansion.

Conclusion

This chapter has presented a framework to understand how certain resource attributes – range of applicability, extent of contractual hazard, and sustainability – affect the direction and mode of diversification. A firm is more likely to diversify into a business: (1) the more applicable is its existing resource pool to that business, (2) the greater the degree to which contractual exploitation of its resource pool in that business is subject to contractual hazards, and (3) the greater the sustainability of the competitive advantage afforded by underlying resources. A firm that diversifies into a new business is more likely to diversify through internal expansion the more applicable its existing resource pool is to that business. Table 3.2 summarizes these effects.

Table 3.2 Summary of effect of resource attributes on diversification patterns

	Effect on direction of diversification	*Effect on mode of diversification*
Existing resource base: range of application	Determines the range of businesses in which the firm is able to gain competitive advantage and earn economic rents	Determines the relative cost/ease/speed with which the firm can build rather than buy resources required to compete in new business
		Determines the extent to which the firm must integrate new business operations into existing operations
Existing resource base: extent of contractual hazards	Determines the feasibility of alternative contractual mechanisms through which the firm can exploit its existing resources	
Existing resource base: sustainability of rents	Determines the attractiveness of competing in the new business	

4   Patent data and construction of a US patent class–SIC concordance

Introduction

Technological prowess is widely perceived to be a fundamental source of corporate and national competitiveness (Patel and Pavitt 1994; Robins and Wiersema 1995). Adherents of the resource-based view of the firm have cited technological competence as a primary firm-specific resource or capability that can propel competitive advantage (Teece 1984; Teece *et al.* 1994). In spite of the prominent role played by technology in the resource-based theoretical framework, however, empirical evidence of technology's role in contouring firms' behavior and performance has remained elusive. This is largely due to difficulties in measuring technological strength, particularly in a manner that will allow the mapping of technological resources or competencies into specific products or industries in which they are likely to be particularly useful. This chapter proposes a method to effect such measurement and mapping.

In the next section of this chapter I briefly describe several measures of technological resources that have been proposed and used in prior theoretical and empirical work, focusing on the advantages and disadvantages associated with each technology measure. I derive from this discussion a set of criteria that an "ideal" measure should satisfy, and argue that patent statistics satisfy a larger subset of these criteria than alternative technology indicators. The third section provides a review of prior research concerning patent statistics in business and economic research, in order to highlight the accomplishments and gaps of the existing literature. In particular, I focus on the inability thus far to link technology, as measured by patents, to relevant downstream product markets. In the fourth section I propose a method for linking US patent classes to the US SIC code at the four-digit level, thus allowing scholars and managers to assess corporate and national patenting trends in terms of the affected industries. This method relies on the use of Canadian patent data and builds on work done by the Yale–Canada Patent Concordance Project in the late 1980s (Kortum and Putnam 1989a, 1989b). I then provide descriptive statistics for the resulting concordance and offer an evaluation of the results for a sample of US patents. The chapter concludes with a brief description of several potential applications for this concordance.

Indicators of technological strength

R&D expenditures

The most frequently used indicator of corporate technological strength in economic and management research has been R&D expenditure. Corporate investment in research and development has been used to proxy for techno-logical skill in studies of corporate performance (Mansfield 1984), diver-sification (Hounshell and Smith 1985; Lemelin 1982), industry profitability (Caves 1987), and research spillovers (Levin and Reiss 1988; Bernstein and Nadiri 1988). Similarly, the innovation games developed by modern industrial organization theorists typically model innovation as a strict function of R&D expenditure, either deterministic (Gilbert and Newbery 1982) or stochastic (Reinganum 1983).[1] R&D investment has the advantage of being reported by all public firms in the US. Nevertheless, the use of R&D spending to measure technological strength suffers from at least two serious drawbacks.

First, R&D spending is an input to, rather than an output of, the innovation process. Any predictions of innovative output based on R&D must therefore rely on an assumption of a strict input–output relationship between R&D and innovation. This assumption may fit well within the framework of neoclassical economics; after all, if the firm is essentially a "black box" that converts inputs into outputs, and new technological discoveries are drawn from a pool that is equally available to all firms willing to invest, then measurement of the inputs to innovation provides almost as much information as measurement of outputs would. However, empirical research suggests significant variability in the ability of firms to convert R&D into meaningful technological results. Several scholars have demonstrated variations in the results of R&D as a function of industry, firm size and other characteristics (e.g., Freeman 1982). Others have noted firm-specific differences in returns to R&D (Lev and Sougiannis 1993). Further, one of the primary inspirations behind the resource-based framework is the desire explicitly to incorporate and explain persistent firm heterogeneity. If firms are heterogeneous, then it is unreasonable to assume that they are homogeneous in their ability to convert R&D into innovations.[2]

The second drawback to using R&D as an indicator of technological output is methodological. Except for information collected by the Federal Trade Com-mission (FTC) on business units of large US businesses for four years in the 1970s (US Federal Trade Commission 1973, 1974, 1975, 1976), publicly avail-able corporate R&D expenditures are almost never disaggregated by lines of business. Thus, while I would expect very different results if a firm devoted its annual research budget equally across all 20 two-digit manufacturing SICs than if it targeted the same budget entirely to one business, studies that rely on R&D investment cannot identify these different research strategies. The one excep-tion to this, in which Scott and Pascoe (1987) used the above-mentioned FTC line of business data to determine whether firms pursue different research strategies, found that many firms do indeed appear to follow "purposively diversified" research strategies. This is further evidence that firm-wide R&D statistics are not adequate measures of technological resources, at least for research questions in which the distribution of R&D expenditure across fields of endeavor is important.[3]

A final drawback to R&D expenditures is that they are not publicly available for all companies. Public companies headquartered in the United States are required by law to publish their annual R&D expenditures. However, most private firms and foreign firms do not provide statistics on R&D in any regularly produced and verifiable manner. The lack of consistent information for these firms can severely proscribe the generalizability of much empirical work based on R&D spending.

Scientific personnel

Another measure of corporate R&D inputs focuses on scientific personnel rather than monetary expenditure. Several scholars (Gort 1962; Mowery 1983) have measured a firm's technological intensity as the ratio of its scientific or research employees to its total employment. Such a measure may be less subject than R&D expenditure to short-term fluctuations. However, it suffers from the same weaknesses as R&D spending: (1) the R&D employment ratio is an input to, rather than an output of, the innovative process, and (2) R&D employment figures tend to be firm-wide rather than specific to component businesses, thus making it impossible to identify line of business research efforts. Finally, data concerning corporate personnel are typically much more difficult to collect than are R&D investment figures.[4]

Innovation counts

An alternate measure of technological strength is the identification of innovations generated by a firm or an industry. Innovation-based measures of technology have been used in studies of the sources of technological change (Pavitt 1984, and other SPRU studies), the technological diversity of firms (Pavitt *et al.* 1989), the relationship between technological change and industry life cycle (Gort and Klepper 1982), and the role of technological opportunity on new business generation (Acs *et al.* 1994). Innovation-based measures of technology have several advantages over R&D spending. First, innovations represent outputs of the innovation process rather than inputs, and as such are more closely aligned with technological resources developed by firms. Second, innovations can be categorized by industry of application, thus identifying specific businesses in which firms' technological strengths are concentrated. Further, with sufficient expertise on the part of the identifiers, innovations can be categorized by their technological or economic importance (i.e., into "major" and "minor" innovations) to further refine the measurement of a firm's technological strength.

Innovation identification also suffers from two drawbacks, both methodological. First, innovation announcements are not regularly published or compiled in any public form. Compilation of innovation statistics is therefore a particularly uncertain process, subject to omissions and inconsistencies in their identification and extremely vulnerable to biases in favor of successes.[5] Second, and relatedly, innovation identification is a laborious and costly process. Gort and Klepper traced important innovations through an intensive primary and secondary source method that entailed directly contacting scores of firms in their sample. Similarly, Edwards and Gordon's (1984) study of innovation in the US during 1982, commissioned by the US Small Business Administration, entailed the search of over a hundred trade journals for innovation announcements, followed by thousands of telephone calls to collect additional information from the innovators. The most comprehensive innovation identification study, carried out by SPRU, required the participation of hundreds of experts and the surveying of thousands of individuals over a 15-year period.

Patents and patent statistics

Given the limitations associated with the above-described indicators of technological resources, it is not surprising that "patents and patent statistics have fascinated economists for a long time" (Griliches 1990: 1661). Scholars have used patent data to study relationships between R&D spending and inventive output (Pakes and Griliches 1984; Griliches *et al.* 1987; Scherer 1982a), to estimate stock market valuation of technological output (Pakes 1985), to explore characteristics of R&D spillovers (Jaffe 1986, 1988, 1989b), to assess the effect of economic conditions on technological output at the industry level (Schmookler 1962a, 1966, 1972), and to measure technological "competence" at the corporate and national levels (Pavitt 1982, 1985; Patel and Pavitt 1987, 1994; Narin *et al.* 1987). In addition, many scholars have researched patents with the explicit intention of estimating the validity of patent statistics as technological indicators (Comanor and Scherer 1969; Carpenter *et al.* 1981; Trajtenberg 1990).

What exactly are included in patent statistics? In the United States, the US Patent and Trademark Office (USPTO) issues patents for inventions that meet a certain minimum standard of novelty and utility.[6] Approximately 100,000 patent applications are filed annually, and approximately 65 percent are eventually granted (Griliches 1990).[7] In the course of examining a patent application to determine whether or not to grant it, a patent examination officer assigns it to a technology-based patent class within the US Patent Classification System. The officer also compiles a list of all previously awarded patents on which the current application relies, known as references or citations by the current patent. If the patent is granted, then the USPTO publishes a patent document, which makes all of the above information part of the public record.[8]

As Table 4.1 shows, among the information provided on the front page of a patent are the date on which the patent application was filed, the company or

Table 4.1 Information available on the front page of US patents (2)

Patent number
Title
Application date
Grant date
Inventor(s)
State/country of inventor(s)
Assignee
Type of applicant (individual, non-profit, for-profit private, government)
US patent class (USPC)
International patent class (IPC)
US references
Foreign references
References to publications
Abstract
Claims

---

other organization to which the patent was assigned upon granting,[9] the patent classification assigned, and the citation list added by the patent officer. Patent documents thus offer a great deal of valuable information concerning the type of innovations that have been developed (patent class), who has developed them (assignee), when they were developed (date of application),[10] and on what prior art they rely (citations). While other information has been used in a few studies – notably the geographic location of inventors (Jaffe *et al.* 1993) – most research has focused on these four fields.

Compared to R&D statistics, then, patents provide richer information on corporate technological resources. Further, patent statistics provide information by technology-based patent class, which is a much more finely grained measure of technological resources than are firm-wide R&D figures. For example, with patent statistics one can discern that Motorola has the bulk of its technological resources concentrated in communications, computing, and various electronics technologies, while Johnson and Johnson's portfolio of patents is skewed towards pharmaceuticals, detergents, and chemicals. These differences between Motorola's and Johnson and Johnson's technological arsenals, which arguably have significant ramifications for these firms' competitive positions, are obscured by aggregate R&D statistics.

Compared to innovation counts, patents are (1) inexpensive to collect and (2) follow a consistent policy of information disclosure. Scholars and policy-makers need not spend the time and money necessary to conduct an exhaustive innovation identification survey. In addition, as Kuznets (1962) points out, patent data implicitly ensure that the innovations identified must meet some minimum standard of technological and economic value: "A patent is presumably issued after a test has been made of an invention's technological soundness ... Furthermore, since it takes time and money to secure a patent, its issuance is evidence that someone ... believes that the potential economic value of the patent warrants the expenditure."

Along with these advantages associated with patent data, it is necessary to recognize their limitations. Three major problems with patent data have been raised and debated over the last three decades: the fact that patents do not (and indeed cannot) encompass all technological resources or inventive output,[11] the wide variation in technological and economic importance embodied in individual patents, and the difficulty in classifying patents according to an industry-based categorization. Indeed, some have argued that these problems introduce sufficient noise into patent statistics that scholars should give up trying to use them at all, a position that sparked much lively debate in the 1960s. An example of this can be found in the following exchange from the proceedings of a National Bureau of Economic Research conference, "The Rate and Direction of Inventive Activity," from 1962:

> In this century a number of students have attempted to use [patents] as a possible measure of inventiveness, inventive activity, or other related concepts. The most persistent of this group has been Jacob Schmookler, who has argued at length and repeatedly that patent statistics are … a useful measure of inventive activity. Schmookler has drawn many conclusions about inventive activity from patent data. Unfortunately, these conclusions and assertions are not supported by valid empirical evidence, and in the opinion of this author they are unwarranted and unsound … In general, the patent data are widely variable and cannot form the basis of serious research.
>
> (Sanders 1962: 69)

> No one will dispute that accurate measures of a thing are always better than an uncertain *index* of it. There is just one difficulty. While we have the uncertain index, we do not have accurate measures … When such data as Sanders prefers are available, I shall be the first to abandon patent statistics in their favor. In the meantime, much as we might prefer caviar, we had better settle for plain bread when that is all we can get.
>
> (Schmookler 1962b: 78)

In general, however, students of innovation have agreed with Schmookler's contention that "we have a choice of using patent statistics cautiously and learning what we can from them, or not using them and learning nothing about what they alone can teach us" (1966: 56).

The fact that patents do not capture all innovations and that systematic differences in the comprehensiveness of patenting may exist across firms, industries, and time has been noted by numerous authors. First, not all innovations are patentable (Griliches *et al.* 1987; Patel and Pavitt 1994). Second, patents in different technologies and businesses may offer varying levels of protection. The extent to which a patent may offer a strong appropriability regime (Teece 1986) and consequently deter imitation (Mansfield *et al.* 1981) plays a large part in an innovator's decision whether or not to patent its patentable technology. Finally, different firms (or the same firm at different points in time) may employ different patenting strategies that result in different propensities to patent.[12]

In response to this criticism of patent data, Patel and Pavitt (1994) have argued that codified (patented) knowledge and uncodified (unpatented and perhaps unpatentable) knowledge are highly complementary. To support this, they point out that other measures of technological competence that incorporate tacit knowledge, such as judgments by technological "peer" experts, have been shown to yield similar results to those of patent measures (Patel and Pavitt 1987; Pavitt 1982; see also Narin *et al.* 1987, as well as Irvine and Martin 1983 on converging indicators). Jaffe's research on R&D spillovers within and between technology "clusters" based on corporate patent portfolios is also consonant with this assertion of complementarity. Thus, while patents do not directly measure a firm's non-codifiable knowledge, there is reason to believe that they may serve as a partial, noisy indicator of its unpatentable technological resources.

As for differing propensities to patent, Mansfield *et al.* (1981: 173) sought to determine "to what extent do firms make use of the patent system, and what differences exist among firms and industries and over time in the propensity to patent?" He conducted extensive surveys of 100 large US firms, all with high levels of R&D spending, whose primary businesses were distributed across 12 two-digit industries. For each firm, Mansfield obtained an estimate of the percentage of its patentable inventions developed between 1981 and 1983 that were patented. These percentages varied, but except for primary steel products (50 percent) and motor vehicles (65 percent), all other industries surveyed had patenting propensities between 75 percent and 86 percent.

As numerous scholars have also pointed out, "the size or value of the 'output' associated with a particular patent varies considerably over patents" (Pakes and Griliches 1980; see also Scherer 1965; Kuznets 1962; Pavitt 1982). Some patents offer only marginal incremental improvements over prior art, frequently with limited economic value,[13] while others offer tremendous technological and/or economic value. Recent empirical evidence based on a variety of sources has quantified the dispersion in economic value of patents. In most European countries, patent owners have long been required to pay annual patent renewal fees during the patent's lifetime.[14] This has yielded a convenient database with which to estimate the variation in (and rate of obsolescence of) economic value of European patents; presumably a patent owner will continue to pay the renewal fee only as long as the expected return to owning the patent right exceeds the fee payment. Pakes and Schankerman (1984), Schankerman and Pakes (1986), and Pakes (1986) have used this data to demonstrate the wide dispersion in economic value of patents, finding that 1 percent of European patents are worth more than $70,000, while most of the remaining patents are almost worthless, yielding a mean value of $7000. This underscores the difficulty of relying too heavily on patent statistics, especially simple patent counts. After all, the fact that firm X has more patents than firm Y says little about the two firms' relative technological resource positions if firm

Y's patents, though fewer in number, are of greater technological or economic importance.

Once again, however, the limitation on patent data implied by variation in patent values should not be overstated. First, as Kuznets recognized, while variation across patents might prevent scholars from interpreting simple patent counts at the margin, at some level of magnitude these counts must still offer insight:

> To use an extreme illustration: if one patent is issued in area A and one thousand in area B, we could hardly conclude that the output of new inventions, measured by their potential economic contribution, is not larger in area B than in area A ... It should be possible to interpret patent statistics [for large volumes of patents] as meaningful indexes of the output of inventive activity – despite the wide range in the economic contribution of individual patents or variations in the averages of large groups.
>
> (Kuznets 1962: 39)

In addition, it is possible to use more sophisticated patent statistics to ameliorate the difficulties posed by variations in their quality. A recent and growing body of literature suggests that patent citation data can yield information on cited patents' value. In an early study in this vein, Carpenter *et al.* (1981) compared the citation rate for 100 technologically significant patents issued in 1969/1970 against that of 102 randomly selected control patents from the same time period. They found that these significant patents were cited more than twice as frequently as the control patents – a statistically significant difference (Carpenter *et al.* 1981; National Science Board 1991).[15] Subsequent studies by these authors and their colleagues have found additional evidence to support the contention that the frequency with which a patent is cited is highly correlated with its technological importance, and that a firm's citation-weighted patent statistics are correlated with independent evaluations of its relative technological strength and financial performance (Narin *et al.* 1987; Frame and Narin 1990). In related research, Trajtenberg (1990) has found a high correlation between patent citation rates and independent estimates of the patented innovations' social economic value in computer tomography.

Thus, while variation in quality among patents raises questions about uncritical reliance on patent statistics, recent research suggests that these questions can be fruitfully addressed. Cautious interpretation of patent counts, coupled with more sophisticated patent citation information, can still yield insight into technological change and into corporate or national technological competence.

Comparison to an "ideal" measure of technological resources

To sum up, the above discussion has uncovered several criteria that an ideal measure of technological resources would satisfy (see Table 4.2). This ideal indicator would operationalize technological know-how as an output, not an

Table 4.2 Summary of relative advantages of various technological resource measures

	Ideal measure	R&D intensity	Scientific personnel	Innovation counts	Patent statistics	Citation-wgtd patent stats.
Appropriateness of technology measure						
Measures technological outputs (not inputs)	+	0	0	+	+[a]	+
Measures technological resources in well-defined units	+	+	+	0	0	0/+
Comprehensive measurement of all technological resources	+	0	0	0	0	0
Provision of microanalytic detail						
Measures individual elements of technological resources	+	0	0	+	+	+
Provides well-defined range of applications for technological resources	+	0	0	+[b]	+	+
Reveals magnitude of advance embodied by technological resources	+	0	0	+[b]	0	+
Feasibility of data collection						
Data collection is inexpensive/costless	+	+	0	0	+	+
Data is publicly available (for all firms)	+	0	0	0	+	+

Notes
a Although there is evidence to suggest that non-citation-weighted patents are "intermediate" between inputs and outputs (Pavitt 1985).
b This depends on the level of detail in the innovation identification survey.

input, of the research process. The indicator would capture all elements of such technological know-how (codified and uncodified), and would do so in terms of a well-defined unit of measure. Further, this indicator would provide extremely detailed information regarding the attributes of each unit of technological resource, particularly with respect to the resource's specific range of potential applications and the magnitude of the advance embodied therein. Finally, of course, this ideal indicator would be costless and universally available for all firms. Not surprisingly, no indicator currently exists that satisfies all of these requirements. Given the present alternatives, patent data remain perhaps the most attractive measure of technological resources currently available.

Linking patents to industries of application

The earliest large-scale attempt to link patents to relevant SIC codes was undertaken by Schmookler in the late 1950s. Schmookler sought to determine whether invention "leads or lags demand conditions" (Schmookler 1966). Using patent application statistics as his measure of invention, Schmookler found that, in many industries, shifts in demand preceded changes in patenting behavior. He interpreted this to suggest that, contrary to the prevailing wisdom of the time, innovation was driven by demand more than by the internal work-ings of technology.

Since the demand conditions of concern to Schmookler were for downstream products rather than for underlying technologies, a prerequisite for his work was a method for categorizing patents by their industries of use.[16] Schmookler's solu-tion was to assign USPTO subclasses to specific industries, where possible. The assignment of patent subclasses was problematic because, even at the relatively specific technical–functional level of a single subclass, patents might have widely disparate industrial applications.[17] To overcome this obstacle, Schmookler combed through the USPTO's patent subclass list, assigning to specific four-digit SIC industries those subclasses for which either (1) the names suggested uniform assignment or, failing that, where (2) at least two-thirds of a random sample of patents from the subclass were judged by Schmookler to fall within a single industry. Using this technique, Schmookler was able to assign approximately 10,000 subclasses (out of more than 50,000 in the US Patent Classification system at that time) to 88 four-digit industries. Schmookler was forced to exclude the remaining 40,000 subclasses as "excessively heterogeneous." "One deficiency of the data is that an undetermined number of the patents relating to the industries are omitted . . . On the other hand . . . while the series are in some measure incomplete, they are relatively pure" (1966: 22–23).

Schmookler's attempt to link patents to industries by concording patent sub-classes to SIC codes was an awe-inspiring endeavor, made all the more remark-able by the fact that it was done before the advent of computerization. Nevertheless, this linkage is of limited utility for several reasons. First, the inability to assign 80 percent of all patent subclasses precludes one from apply-ing the Schmookler concordance to the vast majority of US patenting activity.

Similarly, the exclusion of several hundred four-digit SIC industries makes the concordance inapplicable to significant portions of the economy. Finally, such a concordance requires at least occasional realignment. It is not clear for how many years the Schmookler concordance remained an accurate depiction of technology–industry relations in the US; certainly by the 1990s it is obsolete, and updating would essentially require a dedicated analyst to start from scratch. It is perhaps telling that no major study of patents has used Schmookler's concordance since his last study in 1972.

In the late 1970s, F.M. Scherer attempted to trace flows of technology through the US economy by identifying the industry of origin and industries of use for patented technologies (Scherer 1982a, 1984a, 1984b). Scherer and several of his graduate students selected a sample of 443 large US corporations, and obtained a copy of every patent issued to these firms during a nine-month period from 1976–1977. This resulted in a sample of 15,112 patents – 61 percent of all patents issued to US corporations during that period. The study team members then read each patent document to determine its industry of origin and up to three industries of use.[18] They found, among other things, evidence to suggest that a large proportion of the benefit from new patented technologies is appropriated by downstream users (Scherer 1982a).[19]

As with Schmookler's work, Scherer's effort to link patents to industries of use is awe-inspiring. The detailed assignment of more than 15,000 patents on an individual basis likely provides the most accurate linkage to date of US patents to industries. Unfortunately, it is difficult to generalize from Scherer's work to a broad patent–industry concordance. While one might assemble the Scherer patent sample by patent class and use the resulting patent class–line of business relationships as the basis for mapping patent classes into industrial classes, two obstacles exist. First, while Scherer's patent sample is enormous, given the individual attention involved, it is a fairly small base on which to found a concordance. More daunting is the dating of the study. The Scherer patent–industry linkage is based on patents granted nearly twenty years ago. It is unlikely that the same relations between patent classes and industries (or between industries of origin and industries of use, for that matter) remain in effect today, and there is no way to "update" the Scherer linkages except to again start from scratch.

Recognizing the potential utility of the ability to map patents into industries, in 1981 the USPTO unveiled a concordance between the US Patent Classification system and the US SIC system. Following Schmookler, the USPTO's Office of Technology Assessment and Forecasting (OTAF) assigned patent subclasses to SIC codes, but at the $2\frac{1}{2}$ digit level rather than at the four-digit level. Those patent subclasses that did not belong exclusively to one SIC industry were counted in all relevant industries.

The OTAF concordance provided another reasonable approach to linking patents to industries, but it too was afflicted with weaknesses. Critics lamented both the "arbitrariness in the assignment of some of the subclasses and the misleading inferences that could arise from the pervasive double-counting"

(Griliches 1990). An example of the latter, detailed by Soete (1983), was that concordance-based data analysis showed significant and increasing patenting by Japanese firms in aircraft during the late 1970s. This proved to be an artifact of double-counting, as the "engines" patent subclass, in which the Japanese had a strong presence due to automobile engine patents, was assigned to aircraft as well as automobiles. As an indication of the former – or at least as an indication of the errors present in the concordance – Scherer compared the OTAF concordance's prediction of SIC of application to that assigned to individual patents by his team for a quasi-random sample of 99 patents drawn from his larger sample of 15,112 patents.[20] Scherer found that the OTAF concordance assignments of these patents corresponded with his at the two-digit SIC level for 62 of the patents (63 percent of all cases), and corresponded at the three-digit level for 50 of the patents (51 percent of all cases). While differences in the goals and context of Scherer's work and the OTAF concordance may explain some of the discrepancies, the lack of greater consensus between the two data sources has worried many scholars and policy-makers (Griliches 1990; OTAF 1985).

A further disadvantage of the OTAF concordance is its relatively high level of aggregation. Since it assigns patents only at the two- and three-digit levels, the concordance assignments cannot support as finely grained research as could prior linkages.

In sum, then, several problems have plagued the development of a patent class–SIC linkage of use to scholars, managers, and policy-makers. Given the disjoint relationship between the technical/functional basis of patent classification and products or industries, attempts to link entire classes of patents to a limited number of industries are destined to encompass high degrees of error. Further, such concordances will likely become increasingly disconnected from reality over time, without regular and costly updating. On the other hand, individual patent assignment to applicable SICs is extremely costly and labor-intensive for scholars. As Griliches has pointed out, "one way to get around some of these problems is to have the patent examiner assign the individual patent to one or several SIC industries" (1990: 1667). Unfortunately, the USPTO has shown little inclination to add this burden to those already shouldered by its patent officers. However, the patent officers in the Canadian Patent Office have assigned individual patents issued in that country to relevant Canadian SIC industries at the four-digit level since the late 1970s. It is possible to employ this Canadian data as the basis for a US patent class–US SIC concordance that will overcome many of the weaknesses that have plagued prior efforts at such a linkage.

The construction of a US patent–SIC concordance, via Canada

The Canada Patent Office's PATDAT database

In the mid-1970s, in response to proposals outlined in several government and private sector reports,[21] the Canada Patent Office initiated a project whereby it collected and developed unusually extensive information on each patent granted in Canada. The new database, called PATDAT, was designed with the explicit intention of facilitating economic analysis of patents, technological trends, and the implications of Canadian patent policies.[22] Toward this end, PATDAT includes for almost all patents the likely four-digit Canadian SIC of use and, if applicable, the likely four-digit SIC of manufacture for the patented technology.[23] The PATDAT project includes all patents issued in Canada from 1978 through 1993.

The assignment of SIC information to individual Canadian patents is done by the Canadian Patent Office (CPO). Much like its US counterpart, the CPO employs patent examination officers who, upon granting a patent, assign it to a technology/function-based patent class. These officers are generally experts in particular technological areas. The PATDAT project required that they be trained by members of the Standards Branch of Statistics Canada, the government agency that administers Canada's SIC system, to accurately associate patents with SICs. A small pilot project demonstrated the feasibility (and presumably the accuracy) of patent examination officers' effecting the individual assignment of patents to SICs. Patent officers assign each granted patent to at least one SIC of use.[24] If the patent is for a product, then the patent officer also records at least one SIC of manufacture.[25] If the patent is for a process, then the idea of an industry of manufacture is not meaningful, and none is assigned. Table 4.3 lists the information available through PATDAT.

Thus Canada's patent data since 1978 is linked to relevant SIC codes of use and manufacture. Unlike the OTAF concordance system in the US, Canada's patent–SIC assignments are made manually on a patent-by-patent basis. As Ellis (1981) points out, this has advantages and disadvantages, but the former outweigh the latter. The Canadian system, due to its reliance on individual classification, is subject to human error and individual officer subjectivity. On the other hand, considering each patent on an individual basis greatly reduces the misassignment of patents in heterogeneous patent classes. In addition, any class-based concordance system will presumably require periodic costly and

Table 4.3 Information available in the Canada PATDAT patent database

---

Patent number
Application date
Grant date
Inventor(s)
Province(s)/country(ies) of inventor(s)
Patentee*
Type of applicant (individual, company, government)
Type of patent (product, process, cost-reducing, non-cost reducing)
International patent class (IPC)
Canadian SIC of use
Canadian SIC of manufacture

Note
*Equivalent to Assignee in US parlance.

time-consuming revisions. This may be due to obvious changes, such as revision of the SIC system or the patent classification system. The concordance system is also subject to a more pernicious obsolescence due to changes in the underlying relationship between technologies and product markets. For example, the "digital convergence" of the last decade implies that some digital technologies, once the province solely of computing products, are now also highly applicable to communications. Without revision, the OTAF concordance cannot recognize and incorporate this shift. However, the individual assignment of patents should naturally incorporate such technological trends.

By virtue of its linkage to the Canadian SIC system, the Canadian patent database can provide students of innovation with an invaluable tool for economic analysis of technology. Several scholars have written favorably of PATDAT (Pavitt 1985; Griliches 1990), but with the exception of largely unpublished work by Evenson and his colleagues, none has attempted to use the data or even explore conceptually its potential.[26] To this author's best knowledge, no research to date has (1) linked the Canadian data to the US SIC system (a prerequisite for conducting economic analysis on patenting within the US) either conceptually or methodologically, (2) attempted to derive empirically and evaluate the PATDAT SIC assignments, or (3) used measures of technological resources derived from PATDAT in economic analyses of corporate, industry, or national economic performance. In the subsequent sections of this chapter I address the first two of these, and in Chapters 5 and 6 I address the third.

Creating a US patent–SIC concordance from PATDAT

In a pair of unpublished papers, Kortum and Putnam (1989a, 1989b) "propose a method to infer patents by industry from observed levels of patenting by technology field." Building on their work, I extend it to allow inference of patenting by industry in other countries using those countries' SIC systems.[27] I then offer empirical evidence to suggest that the model does provide an accurate linkage of patents to US SICs.

Given information on the assignment of some patents to IPC classes, how can one infer the likely industry assignment of other patents? Let us imagine a pool of technology associated with a given IPC code – that is, any patented innovation derived from that pool will be assigned (accurately) to that IPC code. The technologies in that pool will have some underlying "true" distribution across SICs in which they are applicable.[28] As firms or individuals conduct R&D in this technology pool, patents are granted on the resulting innovations. These patents are assigned to the associated IPC and, depending on their use, are (accurately) assigned to the relevant SIC code.

We can easily calculate the frequency distribution of industry assignments for a given IPC based on those patents that have been issued. If we were to select one of these issued patents at random, knowing nothing else about it, then the frequency distribution would serve as a probability distribution for the likely application of that patent. As the number of patents derived from this pool increases, we have more information and (thanks to the law of large numbers) more confidence that the frequency distribution of the granted patents accurately depicts the true distribution of the technology pool itself. If we are confronted with a new patent from this technology pool (and hence assigned to this IPC class) and know nothing else about the new patent, then we can use the frequency distribution for industry assignment of prior patents from this pool to infer industries of application for the new patent. Similarly, if we can assign existing non-Canadian patents to IPC categories, and assume that the underlying distribution of the technology pool is the same within and outside Canada, then we can use the Canadian frequency distributions to map foreign patents into Canadian SICs.

Kortum and Putnam (1989a) model this more formally. Assuming that the J industries partition the set of Canadian SIC industries, that the I patent classes partition the set of IPC assignments, and that each patent is assigned to exactly one SIC and IPC, they define a_{ij} as $P[SIC = j \mid IPC = i]$, the probability that a patent will be assigned to industry j conditional upon its assignment to IPC i. The true underlying distribution across industries of a given IPC class i can then be written as a vector, $a_i = a_{i1}, a_{i2}, \ldots, a_{ij}$, and all vectors a_i can be stacked into a matrix A:

$$
\text{IPC} \begin{array}{c} \text{SIC} \\ \begin{vmatrix} a_{11} & a_{12} & \cdots & a_{1J} \\ a_{21} & \cdots & \cdots & \\ \vdots & & & \\ a_{I1} & \cdots & \cdots & a_{IJ} \end{vmatrix} \end{array}
$$

which describes the probability distribution of industry assignments for any and all possible patent class assignments. As inventors and firms conduct R&D that generates patents, they are essentially sampling (without replacement) from the population of patentable technologies. Kortum and Putnam show that this sampling procedure yields estimates of each a, and of A, that are asymptotically normally distributed. With an increasing number of patents in the sample – in other words, as more patents are granted and assigned to both an IPC and an SIC in Canada – the estimate of A converges in probability to the true A (Kortum and Putnam 1989a).

The above model provides an estimate for the true distribution of the population of patentable technology. This suggests a straightforward method to infer patenting by industry for patents outside of the existing sample, provided that (1) they are assigned to an IPC class, (2) industry assignment by the Canadian SIC system is suitable for the subsequent research, and (3) the cells in matrix A contain a "large" number of observations. One may use the estimate of matrix A to convert any patent assigned to an IPC code – or any vector of patents assigned to IPC codes, either for an entire nation or for a single firm – into probability-weighted industries of application.

Let a firm's patent portfolio be written as a column vector $\mathbf{f} = [f_1, f_2, \ldots, f_I]'$ where f_i = the number of patents owned by the firm that are assigned to IPC i.

Then the firm's patent portfolio can be rewritten in terms of patent-equivalents by industry as follows:

$$[f_1, f_2, \ldots, f_I] \begin{vmatrix} a_{11} & a_{12} & \cdots & a_{1J} \\ a_{21} & \cdots & \cdots & \\ \vdots & & & \\ a_{I1} & \cdots & \cdots & a_{IJ} \end{vmatrix} = [g_1, g_2, \ldots, g_J]$$

where $g_j = \Sigma f_i a_{ij}$.

How useful is such information for US managers and policy-makers? While Kortum and Putnam provide an example of application of the Canadian-based patent-industry matrix to aggregate levels of US chemical patenting, the reliance on Canadian SIC assignment rather than US SIC classification poses a significant obstacle to fruitful application of the PATDAT database outside Canada. Most data used for economic (and managerial) analysis in the US is compiled according to the US SIC system; to the extent that the Canadian system departs from US classification (or, for that matter, from that of any other country), the above-described model is of limited utility.

If one can derive a concordance between Canada's SIC system and that of the US, then one can add to the above model a second matrix that maps Canadian SIC codes into their US equivalents:

$$\text{US SIC}$$

$$\text{Canadian SIC} \begin{vmatrix} b_{11} & b_{12} & \cdots & b_{1K} \\ b_{21} & \cdots & \cdots & \\ \vdots & & & \\ b_{J1} & \cdots & \cdots & b_{JK} \end{vmatrix}$$

where $b_{jk} = P[\text{US SIC} = k \mid \text{Canadian SIC} = j]$.

One could then convert PATDAT data into useful US-based industry data by the following expanded model:

$$[f_1, f_2, \ldots, f_I] \begin{vmatrix} a_{11} & a_{12} & \cdots & a_{1J} \\ a_{21} & \cdots & \cdots & \\ \vdots & & & \\ a_{I1} & \cdots & \cdots & a_{IJ} \end{vmatrix} \begin{vmatrix} b_{11} & b_{12} & \cdots & b_{1K} \\ b_{21} & \cdots & \cdots & \\ \vdots & & & \\ b_{J1} & \cdots & \cdots & b_{JK} \end{vmatrix} =$$

$$[g_1, g_2, \ldots, g_J] \begin{vmatrix} b_{11} & b_{12} & \cdots & b_{1K} \\ b_{21} & \cdots & \cdots & \\ \vdots & & & \\ b_{J1} & \cdots & \cdots & b_{JK} \end{vmatrix} = [h_1, h_2, \ldots, h_K]$$

where $h_k = \Sigma g_j b_{jk}$.

Finally, the USPC system is not identical to the IPC system. As with SIC conversion, if one can map USPCs into IPCs, then one may add to the above model a third matrix that concords USPCs to their IPC equivalents:

$$
\text{USPC} \quad
\begin{array}{c}
\text{IPC} \\
\begin{vmatrix}
z_{11} & z_{12} & \cdots & z_{1I} \\
z_{21} & \cdots & \cdots & \\
\vdots & & & \\
z_{U1} & \cdots & \cdots & z_{UI}
\end{vmatrix}
\end{array}
$$

where $z_{ui} = P[\text{IPC} = i \mid \text{USPC} = u]$.

One could then convert any vector of US patent data $\mathbf{e} = [e_1, e_2, \ldots, e_u]$ to a vector of US industry-based patent-equivalents $\mathbf{h} = [h_1, h_2, \ldots, h_k]$ by:

$$
[e_1, e_2, \ldots, e_u]
\begin{vmatrix}
z_{11} & z_{12} & \cdots & z_{1I} \\
z_{21} & \cdots & & \\
\vdots & & & \\
z_{U1} & \cdots & \cdots & z_{UI}
\end{vmatrix}
\begin{vmatrix}
a_{11} & a_{12} & \cdots & a_{1J} \\
a_{21} & \cdots & & \\
\vdots & & & \\
a_{I1} & \cdots & \cdots & a_{IJ}
\end{vmatrix}
\begin{vmatrix}
b_{11} & b_{12} & \cdots & b_{1K} \\
b_{21} & \cdots & & \\
\vdots & & & \\
b_{J1} & \cdots & \cdots & b_{JK}
\end{vmatrix}
=
$$

$$
[f_1, f_2, \ldots, f_I]
\begin{vmatrix}
a_{11} & a_{12} & \cdots & a_{1J} \\
a_{21} & \cdots & \cdots & \\
\vdots & & & \\
a_{I1} & \cdots & \cdots & a_{IJ}
\end{vmatrix}
\begin{vmatrix}
b_{11} & b_{12} & \cdots & b_{1K} \\
b_{21} & \cdots & \cdots & \\
\vdots & & & \\
b_{J1} & \cdots & \cdots & b_{JK}
\end{vmatrix}
=
$$

$$
[g_1, g_2, \ldots, g_J]
\begin{vmatrix}
b_{11} & b_{12} & \cdots & b_{1K} \\
b_{21} & \cdots & \cdots & \\
\vdots & & & \\
b_{J1} & \cdots & \cdots & b_{JK}
\end{vmatrix}
= [h_1, h_2, \ldots, h_K]
$$

As stated above, this model rests on the assumption that the underlying relationship between technologies and industries of application is the same across the relevant countries – in this case, that the underlying distribution represented by the true matrix **A** in Canada is the same as the underlying distribution in the US. To the extent that this assumption is incorrect, the above model will misassign patents to industries. How heroic is this assumption? It is certainly possible that technology commercialization patterns will systematically differ across nations due to cultural, institutional, or economic differences.[29] For the US and Canada, differences are likely to be negligible. There are few obvious differences between the US and Canada concerning these factors. More important, during the first ten years of PATDAT's collection, more than 50 percent of the patents granted in Canada were granted to US applicants.

A more disturbing concern relates to the noise incorporated in the above model. The conversion of US patents to US SIC-based patent-equivalents entails the use of three separate matrices, each of which is likely to introduce some degree of inaccuracy. While the resulting concordance may offer advantages over previous concordances in level of aggregation and in breadth of coverage, the tradeoff in terms of such inaccuracy is potentially severe. I turn to this issue in the next section, where I attempt to empirically evaluate the results of this concordance.

Empirical results of this model

It is difficult to evaluate any patent–SIC concordance because there is no obviously accurate benchmark against which to measure. One way to estimate the accuracy of a concordance is to compare it to other concordances that are perceived to be reasonably accurate, as Scherer (1982b) did in his comparison of the OTAF concordance's assignment of 99 patents to individual patent assignments made by his research team. In this section I construct a concordance based on the model in the previous section, and compare its assignment of SICs to the 99 patents in Scherer's study.[30] The resulting concordance achieves a much higher correspondence to Scherer's assignments than does the OTAF concordance.

I used PATDAT data for the years 1978–1987, totaling 178,000 patents, to generate an estimate of matrix **A**. This does not directly correspond to the years of the Scherer patents (1976–1977); except for a selective pilot project between 1972 and 1977, the PATDAT data was not compiled before 1978. I included data through the mid-1980s to increase the sample size and consequently obtain robust frequency distributions for **A**. To the extent that the underlying relationship between technology and industry applicability changes markedly over time, inclusion of later years will work against my finding correspondence with Scherer's industry assignments.

I then constructed a matrix **B** to map Canadian SICs into US SICs. Such a mapping could be done in several ways. One method would be to look at activities of multinational corporations operating in both countries to determine how their identical product lines are classified in each. A second method, which was used here, relies on a concordance between the Canada SIC system and the US SIC system, developed by Statistics Canada in conjunction with the US Department of Commerce (Statistics Canada 1990). I assume that this concordance is an accurate, unbiased estimate of the true mapping across SIC systems and incorporate it directly into the above matrix.

If the Canadian SIC system matched the US SIC system on a one-to-one basis – that is, if each Canadian four-digit SIC industry mapped into exactly one US four-digit SIC industry – then this matrix would be composed of 0s and 1s and no other decisions would have to be made.[31] However, if one Canada SIC maps into multiple US SICs, then some rule must be devised to distribute patents assigned to the Canadian SIC across the multiple US SICs. Suppose, for example, that Canadian SIC 1451 is associated with US SICs 2135 and 2136 according to the *Canada SIC–US SIC Concordance*. How shall patents assigned to Canadian SIC 1451 be allocated to these US SICs? One possibility would be to double-count them in each relevant US SIC. However, as described above, double-counting is subject to criticism (Soete 1983). A second possibility would be to divide them equally across the relevant US SICs, so that each patent assigned to Canadian SIC 1451 will be counted as 0.5 patent each in US SICs 2135 and 2136. A third possibility would be to weight the allocation to US SICs by sales, such that if US SIC 2135 accounts for, say, $9 billion in annual sales and US SIC 2136 accounts for $1 billion, each patent assigned to Canadian SIC 1451 will be allocated as 0.9 patent to SIC 2135 and 0.1 patent to SIC 2136. I assigned patents both via equal division across all relevant SICs and via sales-weighted allocation. For the latter, I used 1981 US sales at the four-digit SIC level from the Annual Survey of Manufactures to calculate sales-weightings. Results were similar under both allocation schemes; only sales-weighted results are presented below.

Finally, I dealt with the USPC–IPC conversion issue. As with the SIC concordance, there are several avenues for effecting this mapping. One method would be to identify identical patents filed in both Canada and the US to link their patent class assignments in each country. A second method relies on the *IPC–USPC Concordance* (US Office of Patent Classification Systems 1985), developed by the USPTO, and assumes that this concordance is an accurate, unbiased estimate of the true mapping across patent class systems. A third method is to use the IPC codes directly assigned to US patents by US patent examiners. As Table 4.1 showed, one of the fields completed by patent examiners on the first page of US patents is a relevant IPC assignment. To the extent that these are accurate, their use obviates the need to employ a third matrix.[32] For the evaluation presented here I used both the second and third methods, relying on both the *IPC–USPC Concordance* and on individual patent assignment. The results were nearly identical; only results based on individual assignments are presented below.

I then took each of Scherer's 99 patents in turn as a vector **e**, and determined the US SIC vector **h** associated with that patent. Table 4.4 shows the frequency with which my concordance assigns the patents in this sample to the same SIC as was assigned by Scherer. My concordance provides multiple SICs of likely application, in descending order of probability. There is no hard and fast rule to determine how many of these SICs should be considered viable assignments. It is worth noting that even if one limits the concordance's results to the single most likely SIC for each patent, these correspond to Scherer's assignment almost as well as the OTAF concordance (which can include as many as five different two-digit industry assignments). If one accepts the three most probable SICs of Use and of Manufacture assignments as valid, then the concordance yields the same assignment as Scherer's individual patent assignments at the four-digit level for more than half of the patents, at the three-digit level for more than three-fifths, and at the two-digit level for 83 out of 99 patents.

Table 4.5 provides an alternative way of viewing SIC assignments. Since each SIC assignment has an associated frequency, one may use frequency

Table 4.4 Matches between Scherer and other concordance SIC assignments (based on ranking of SICs in PATDAT concordance) (1)

	OTAF	PATDAT (Top SIC only)*	PATDAT (Top 2 SICs)	PATDAT (Top 3 SICs)	PATDAT (Top 4 SICs)	PATDAT (Top 5 SICs)
Match at four-digit level	n/a	35	49	55	65	68
Match at three-digit level	50	42	53	61	71	72
Match at two-digit level	62	62	76	83	90	91
No match	37	37	23	16	9	8

Note
*"Top SIC only" means that only the most frequently assigned SIC of Use and SIC of Manufacture for a given patent are compared to its Scherer assignment to determine whether there is a match. "Top 2 SICs" means that the two most frequently assigned SICs of Use and SICs of Manufacture for a given patent are compared, etc.

Table 4.5 Matches between Scherer and other concordance SIC assignments (based on relative frequencies of SIC assignments in PATDAT concordance) (2)

	OTAF	PATDAT (P[SIC]/ maxP[SIC]) >= 0.80*	PATDAT (P[SIC]/ maxP[SIC]) >= 0.67	PATDAT (P[SIC]/ maxP[SIC]) >= 0.33	PATDAT (P[SIC]/ maxP[SIC]) >= 0.20	PATDAT (P[SIC]/ maxP[SIC]) >= 0.10
Match at four-digit level	n/a	43	47	53	68	72
Match at three-digit level	50	49	55	61	71	75
Match at two-digit level	62	72	74	76	78	85
No match	37	27	25	23	21	14

Note
*"P[SIC = j]/maxP[SIC] >= 0.80" means that, for a given patent, all SICs of Use (SICs of Manufacture) that are assigned at least 80 percent as frequently as the Top SIC of Use (Top SIC of Manufacture) are compared to the patent's Scherer assignment to determine whether there is a match.

cut-offs rather than ordinal SIC rankings to determine which SICs to consider viable assignments. Again, this concordance provides industry assignments that are highly consonant with those made by Scherer.

Appendix 1 (pp. 96–103) consists of a table that shows the Scherer SIC assignment and the top three assignments by SIC of use and of manufacture derived by my concordance. Examination of this table does not reveal any obvious pattern among those patents for which no match (or just a match at the two-digit level) was found. This may be due in part to the small number of patents involved – with a sample of 99 patents and a "no match" set of 15, it is difficult to discern empirical regularities that might show up in a larger sample. Nevertheless, it is worth noting that patents in the chemical industry (i.e., SIC 283) achieved three- or four-digit matches in a higher proportion than most other areas.[33]

The fact that this concordance yields industry assignments that match Scherer's individual patent assignments more closely than other concordances does not necessarily mean that the concordance is more accurate. It is possible that Scherer's assignments are inaccurate, and that the same biases which lead to inaccuracies in Scherer's research also infuse the Canadian Patent Office's assignment of SICs. However, in the absence of more objective measures of the "true" application of patents to industries, the results presented here indicate that whatever inaccuracy is introduced into the model through use of multiple matrices is more than offset by the increased accuracy of patent–industry assignments afforded by the PATDAT data.

Conclusion

Building on unpublished work from the Yale–Canada Concordance Project, this chapter has provided a new theoretical and empirical method to link US patents to US SICs via the extensive Canadian PATDAT database. I have also conducted an evaluation of such a linkage, finding evidence that my model is more accurate than existing concordances. The concordance demonstrated above should be of great use to scholars of innovation in general and to resource-based theorists in particular. For example, studies of technological competence have assumed that corporate patent portfolios can be translated into competitive advantage. However, in the absence of a mechanism for linking patent portfolios to relevant downstream markets, these studies have been unable to substantiate such claims. This concordance can provide such a mechanism, thus (finally) enabling researchers to trace the effect of upstream technological resources on downstream activities. Chapters 5 and 6 provide empirical tests in this spirit.

5 An empirical analysis of the effect of technological resources on the direction of corporate diversification

Introduction

Previous chapters have argued that a firm's decision to enter new businesses is influenced by the composition of its existing technological resource base and by the extent of transaction costs associated with contracting out its technological resources in potential markets of applicability. This chapter extends this line of reasoning by drawing out hypothetical implications of the above arguments. I then empirically test these hypotheses with data from a stratified sample of entries and non-entries by 412 firms into 429 industries between 1981 and 1985, incorporating a total of 2514 entry and non-entry observations.

Hypotheses

As discussed in Chapters 2 and 3, the resource-based theory rests on two fundamental tenets: (1) firms seek to exploit their rent-producing resources; (2) these rent-producing resources are useful in only a limited range of applications. Technical knowledge, in particular, confers advantage in only a narrow set of businesses (Jaffe 1989a; Patel and Pavitt 1994). Technological resources are therefore likely to prompt patterns of diversification that are far more fine-grained than broad measures of R&D intensity are likely to capture.

H1: Ceteris paribus, a firm will be more likely to diversify into a business the more highly applicable its existing technological resources are to that business.

Resources differ in the extent to which they may be efficiently contracted out. Technological resources, which frequently rest on highly tacit knowledge, are likely to face particularly high market failure risks (Teece 1982; Pisano 1990). Resources related to distribution, such as access to particular channels, are likely to be relatively easy to contract out. Production-related resources are likely to fall somewhere in between technology and distribution resources.

However, differences in contracting hazards may exist even within a particular class of resource. Confining ourselves to technology, certain types of innovations can be more easily licensed than others (Teece 1986). For example, process innovations are commonly perceived to face more significant licensing hazards than product innovations, largely because of difficulties in monitoring their use. Alternatively, different industries may be characterized by varying levels of hazards for contracting out innovations, as implied by the results of the Yale survey of R&D (Levin *et al.* 1987). To the extent that differences exist across technologies or industries in the relative efficiency of contracting for innovations, one would expect to see differences in the diversification patterns of firms who attempt to exploit technology. In particular, transaction cost reasoning suggests that a firm that can efficiently contract out its technological resources into new uses will do so, rather than diversifying to exploit its technological resources.

H2: Ceteris paribus, a firm will be more likely to diversify into a business the more likely that contracting out its technological resources in that business will be subject to high transaction costs.

Not all companies are highly influenced by technology. It is likely that the hypotheses derived above will hold more strongly for those firms that have significant investments in technological resources than for those whose competitive advantage does not rest on technological resources.

H3: A firm's patterns of diversification will be more highly influenced by its technological resources the greater the absolute level of its technological resources.

Specification of the model

The hypotheses enumerated above, concerning the direction of diversification, can be tested in a multivariate binomial logit model of entry into new markets. My model of the direction of diversification borrows from Montgomery and Hariharan (1991).[1] As did they, I look at changes in firm-level diversification as a function of firm characteristics, destination industry characteristics, and the relationship between firm and industry characteristics. I extend their model by including direct measures of the applicability of a firm's technological resource base to potential destination industries as well as measures of the transaction costs associated with contracting out versus in-house exploitation of technological resources.[2] The resulting model appears in Table 5.1.

Data

The research methodology for testing the hypotheses outlined above relies on data derived from eight databases: the AGSM/Trinet Large Establishment database, the US Patent and Trademark Office patent classification database, the Canadian Patent Office's PATDAT database, the Federal Trade Commission's Line of Business data, Compustat, the Census of Manufactures, the Annual Survey of Manufactures, and the Yale survey of research and development prac-

Table 5.1 Model of diversification behavior: direction of diversification

$$P(Div_{ij} = 1) = \beta_0 + \beta_1 ISales_j + \beta_2 IGrowth_j + \beta_3 IConc_j + \beta_4 IR\&DInt_j + \beta_5 IAdvInt_j$$
$$+ \beta_6 FSales_i + \beta_7 FGrowth_i + \beta_8 FR\&DInt_i + \beta_9 FAdvInt_i$$
$$+ \beta_{10} DiffR\&D_{ij} + \beta_{11} DiffAdv_{ij}$$
$$+ \beta_{12} AbsTech_{ij} + \beta_{13} RelTech_{ij}$$
$$+ \beta_{14} Royalty_j + \beta_{15} Secrecy_j + \beta_{16} Learning_j + e_{ij}$$

where:

$P(Div_{ij} = 1)$	The probability that firm i will diversify into industry j
$ISales_j$ ($billion)	Annual sales for industry j
$IGrowth_j$ (%)	CAGR of sales in industry j between 1978 and 1981
$IConc_j$ (%)	4-firm concentration ratio in industry j in 1982
$IR\&DInt_j$ (%)	Industry-wide ratio of R&D expenditure to revenue in 1977
$IAdvInt_j$ (%)	Industry-wide ratio of advertising expenditure to revenue in 1977
$FSales_i$ ($billion)	Sales for firm i in 1981
$FGrowth_i$ (%)*	CAGR of sales by firm i between 1978 and 1981
$FR\&DInt_i$ (%)	Weighted average of the ratio of R&D expenditure to revenue for firm i, 1978–1981
$FAdvInt_i$ (%)	Weighted average of the ratio of advertising expenditure to revenue for firm i in 1978–1981
$DiffR\&D_{ij}$	Absolute value of the difference between industry R&D intensity and firm R&D intensity
$DiffAdv_{ij}$	Absolute value of the difference between industry advertising intensity and firm advertising intensity
$AbsTech_{ij}$	A measure of the applicability of firm i's patent portfolio to industry j in absolute terms
$RelTech_{ij}$	A measure of the applicability of firm i's patent portfolio to industry j, relative to the applicability of firm i's patent portfolio to other industries
$Royalty_j$	Importance of royalties from patent licensing as a mechanism for appropriating returns to innovation in industry j
$Secrecy_j$	Importance of secrecy as a mechanism for appropriating returns to innovation in industry j
$Learning_j$	Importance of coming down a learning curve as a mechanism for appropriating returns to innovation in industry j

tices (see Levin *et al.* 1987). I drew together information on the above-specified firm and industry characteristics for 412 large US firms and 429 four-digit SIC industries in 1981 and 1985.

To generate my sample of firms, I selected a sample of 400 out of the 573 firms included in the database compiled by Adam Jaffe for his research on technological position of firms (1985, 1986, 1988). Jaffe's database included every US firm that (1) reported R&D expenditure in 1976, (2) was granted ten or more patents between 1969 and 1979, and (3) appeared in the Harvard Business School's PICA database for the 1970s. This sample is thus biased toward larger, more technology intensive firms. To offset this bias I also selected a sample of 85 US firms that (1) did not appear in Jaffe's sample and (2) appeared in both Compustat and the AGSM/Trinet databases in 1981. I then eliminated

56 of the Jaffe-derived firms and 17 of the non-Jaffe firms from my sample because they disappeared, either through dissolution or through acquisition, by 1985. The resulting database captures a healthy cross-section of US economic activity, primarily by Fortune 1000 corporations, in the 1981–1985 period (see Appendix 2 on pp. 104–108 for a list of the sample firms).

Figures 5.1, 5.2, and 5.3 show the distribution of the sample firms across several dimensions. The 412 firms in this sample ranged from less than $10 million to more than $100 billion (Exxon) in 1981 sales. As Figure 5.1 indicates, more than half of the firms had 1981 sales of $1 billion or less. It is worth noting, although it is not surprising, that the non-Jaffe firms are overwhelmingly among the smallest in the population, virtually all with sales under $500 million. Sample firms evidenced a similar distribution in the number of four-digit SICs in which they participated, ranging from one SIC (ten firms) to 84 SICs (ITT) with more than half of the firms involved in ten or fewer SICs (see Figure 5.2). Again, the vast majority of non-Jaffe firms appear in the lower half of the distribution. The 412 firms in my sample made a total of 1023 entries between 1981 and 1985. Figure 5.3 indicates the variation in this behavior. Fully one-quarter of these firms made no diversification entries during this period, while one firm (Cooper Industries) diversified into 37 new businesses. Once again, the distribution is skewed toward fewer entries, and this skewness is particularly pronounced for the non-Jaffe firms.

I then constructed patent portfolios for these 412 firms from the US Patent and Trademark Office Patent database. This database includes the front page of every patent granted by the USPTO since 1975. For each firm i in my sample, I identified all patents in the USPTO data that were applied for before December 31, 1981. These patents comprised firm i's patent portfolio, and hence its existing technological resources, as of 1981. Unfortunately, large multiunit firms do

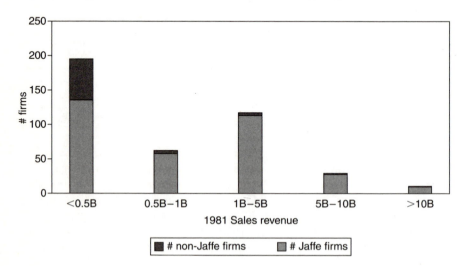

Figure 5.1 Distribution of sample firms by sales.

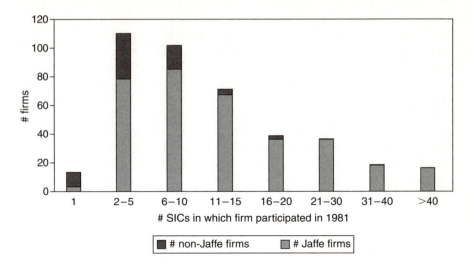

Figure 5.2 Distribution of sample firms by number of SICs.

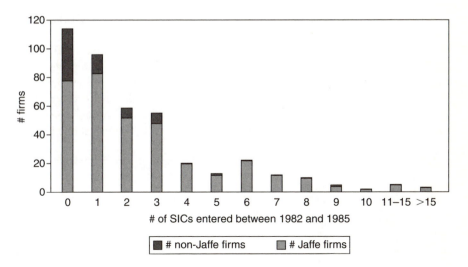

Figure 5.3 Distribution of sample firms by number of entries, 1982–1985.

not always patent under a single consolidated name. It is commonplace for subsidiaries to patent under their names rather than under parent names; indeed, there is anecdotal evidence to suggest that firms deliberately seek to obscure their patent ownership in this way to hinder monitoring efforts by competitors. To address this problem, I used the 1981 *Who Owns Whom*. (Dun and Bradstreet 1981) reference book to identify every subsidiary of each firm in my sample. I then searched the USPTO database for patents assigned to any of these parent or subsidiary names, and aggregated all patents at the parent level.

The resulting patent portfolios varied widely in size, from 0 patents for a few (primarily non-Jaffe) firms to more than 7000 patents for E.I. DuPont. As Figure 5.4 shows, more than half of the sample firms and almost all of the non-Jaffe firms had portfolios of fewer than 50 patents. The firms in this sample accounted for more than 60,000 patents – well over 50 percent of all US patents during this period that were assigned to organizations – assigned to more than 1,500 patenting entities.

For my sample of industries, I compiled information on all four-digit SIC manufacturing industries – that is, all 449 four-digit SIC industries between SIC 2000 and SIC 3999.[3] I then eliminated 20 industries for which information (frequently advertising intensity or R&D intensity; occasionally growth or concentration) was not available, yielding a final set of 429 potential destination industries.

The dependent variable

The dependent variable, Div_{ij}, is derived from the AGSM/Trinet Large Establishment database (Trinet) and is coded as a categorical variable:

$Div_{ij} = 1$ if firm i enters industry j between 1981 and 1985, and 0 otherwise.

The Trinet data was compiled for every odd-numbered year between 1979 and 1989 by an eponymous market research company.[4] The Trinet database includes information on corporate ownership, employment, and four-digit SIC code of operations (as well as other characteristics not relevant to the current study) for over 400,000 establishments in the United States. Through the use of several secondary sources and millions of telephone calls, Trinet claimed it was

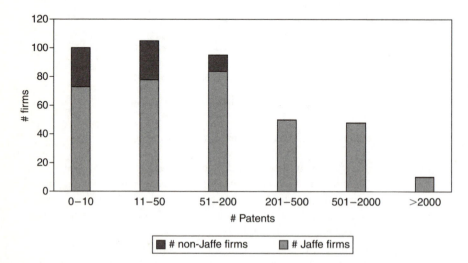

Figure 5.4 Distribution of sample firms by size of patent portfolio.

able to collect information on virtually every establishment with 20 or more employees in the United States. Subsequent studies by scholars and Census of Manufactures employees suggest that Trinet achieved a better than 95 percent accuracy level in its efforts.[5] For establishments in which more than one four-digit SIC business is undertaken, Trinet provides up to three separate SIC codes (with SIC-specific employee breakdowns). Studies by researchers at the Census of Manufactures suggest that less than 3 percent of all US manufacturing establishments contained more than three four-digit SIC operations during the 1980s (see, for example, Streitwieser 1991: 507).

Thanks to the presence of corporate parentage information for each plant, it is possible to identify all establishments of a given parent firm in the Trinet data. By aggregating the Trinet establishment data at the firm level, I determined all four-digit SICs in which my 412 firms participated in 1981 and in 1985. Any industry in which firm i does not participate in 1981 is a potential destination industry in 1985. Those potential destination industries in which firm i does participate in 1985 are entries, and are coded as 1. Those potential destination industries in which firm i does not participate in 1985 are non-entries, and are coded as 0. Entry occurred in 1023 of the 170,721 potential entries in my sample (0.5 percent),[6] and non-entry occurred in 169,698 (99.4 percent) of the potential entries.

The independent variables

The independent variables were constructed as follows:

New operationalizations of technological resources

AbsTech$_{ij}$ is defined as the absolute level of firm i's patent portfolio that is likely to be applicable to industry j. It is derived from the US Patent and Trademark Office database and the Canadian Patent Office database as follows. First, as described above, I compiled firm i's US patent portfolio by identifying all patents assigned to firm i, or any of firm i's subsidiaries, that were applied for on or before December 31, 1981 and that were granted after 1975. Second, using the US patent class–US SIC concordance developed in Chapter 4, I derived probability-weighted assignments to four-digit SICs for each patent in firm i's portfolio. Finally, I aggregated these probability-weighted SICs over firm i's entire patent portfolio to determine the total strength of firm i's technological resources, as measured by patents, in each SIC. This measure of industry-specific technological strength is AbsTech$_{ij}$:

$$\text{AbsTech}_{ij} = \sum_{c} \text{Prob}(\text{industry} = j \mid \text{patent} = c) * N_{ic}$$

where N_{ic} equals the number of patents in firm i's portfolio that are assigned to US patent class c.

As was described in Chapter 4, the conversion of Canadian SICs to US SICs can be done either with or without sales-weighting. For this empirical test I constructed absolute technological applicability measures using both weighted and unweighted concordance values. These measures are called $WgtAbsTech_{ij}$ and $UnwgtAbsTech_{ij}$, respectively. It is a primary contention of this thesis that a precise specification of a firm's resources – particularly the range of their applicability – will significantly improve the explanatory power of resource-based theory. Toward that end, Hypothesis 1 proposes that a firm is more likely to diversify into an industry if its technological resources are highly applicable to that industry. The coefficient for the applicability of firm i's patent portfolio to industry j (in absolute terms) is therefore expected to be positive; a positive, significant coefficient will be interpreted as support for Hypothesis 1.[7]

$RelTech_{ij}$ is defined as the applicability of firm i's patent portfolio to industry j, relative to the applicability of firm i's patent portfolio to other industries. For a firm with a large patent portfolio, absolute measures of technological applicability will yield large values for many industries. While such measures capture some sense of firm i's technological strength in industry j, they do not provide any information on firm i's technological strength in industry j as compared with firm i's strength in other industries that it could potentially enter. $RelTech_{ij}$ measures this relative attractiveness of industry j. It is derived from the absolute patent portfolio applicability measures described above as follows:

$$WgtRelTech_{ij} = WgtAbsTech_{ij}/\max_j\{WgtAbsTech_{ij}\}$$
$$UnwgtRelTech_{ij} = UnwgtAbsTech_{ij}/\max_j\{UnwgtAbsTech_{ij}\}$$

The coefficient for relative technological applicability is expected to be positive, and will also be interpreted as support for Hypothesis 1.

Industry variables

$ISales_j$ is defined as the total annual sales of industry j in \$ billion in 1981. It is taken directly from the *Annual Survey of Manufactures* for 1981. The level of industry sales is not commonly used as an independent variable in studies of entry, because the size of a destination industry has not played a large role in classical entry barrier theory. I include industry sales for a different reason. As many scholars have noted, the SIC system is not constructed in an ideal fashion (Davis and Duhaime 1992). Consequently, some SIC codes are likely to encompass more than one "true" business. The industry sales measure should capture the fact that if one SIC code happens to include a larger part of the economy than another, then a firm's diversification is more likely to show up in that SIC code. Thus, the coefficient for industry sales is expected to be positive.

$IGrowth_j$ is measured as the compound annual growth rate of total sales in SIC j between 1978 and 1981. It is derived from the industry sales figures available in the *Annual Survey of Manufactures* for 1978 and 1981.[8] The traditional entry barrier framework suggests that higher industry growth will encourage entry. When an industry is growing, an entrant's production is less likely to elicit strong responses from incumbents and thus is less likely to depress prices and profits (Orr 1974). Conversely, stagnant industry growth often precedes an increase in industry rivalry, which can deter entry (Porter 1980). The coefficient for industry growth is therefore expected to be positive.

$IConc_j$ is measured as the four-firm concentration ratio for industry j in 1982.[9] This measure is available from the *Census of Manufactures*, which is compiled by the US Commerce Department every five years. The four-firm concentration ratio typically does not change significantly from one year to another, so any misspecification incurred by using a 1982 figure in conjunction with other data compiled for 1981 should be negligible. Classical entry barrier theory typically considers high concentration a barrier to entry, in that established firms are positioned to collude to deter entry. Thus, the coefficient for industry concentration is expected to be negative.

$IR\&DS_j$ – R&D intensity for industry j – is measured as the industry-wide ratio of R&D expenditure to total revenue in 1976. This ratio was available from the Federal Trade Commission's *Statistical Report: Line of Business Activity*, which compiled information at the Line of Business level for roughly 350 of the largest US firms between 1973 and 1976. There is no publicly available source of industry-wide R&D intensity that is contemporaneous with the rest of my 1981–1985 data. However, it is generally believed that the level of industry-wide R&D intensity does not change significantly over a five-year period, so the use of 1976 data for a 1981 empirical test may not introduce too much noise.[10] High R&D intensity is traditionally proposed to be a barrier to entry. However, Montgomery and Hariharan (1991) suggest that it is effective as a barrier only against smaller, newer firms. Indeed, their empirical work suggests that large firms that already maintain high investments in R&D in their existing businesses might be attracted to high-R&D destination industries precisely because competitive advantage in such industries relies on R&D-related resources. Since my sample of firms generally includes larger, technology intensive firms, I expect the coefficient for industry R&D intensity to be positive, if it is significant at all. If this sample included predominantly small, young (or *de novo*) firms, then one would expect the coefficient to be negative, as predicted by traditional entry barrier theory.

$IAdvS_j$ – advertising intensity for industry j – is measured as the industry-wide ratio of advertising expenditure to total revenue in 1976. As was industry R&D intensity, this ratio was available from the Federal Trade Commission's *Statistical Report: Line of Business Activity* and is subject to the same criticisms concerning lack of contemporaneous data. Like R&D intensity, high industry advertising intensity is traditionally viewed as a barrier to entry but is likely to be ineffective or even an inducement for certain firms to enter when potential entrants are large, diversifying firms. Given my sample, the coefficient for industry-wide advertising intensity is thus expected to be positive, if it is significant at all.

Firm variables

FSales$_i$ is defined as the total annual sales of firm i in $ billion in 1981. It is taken directly from the Compustat database. Prior work in this area has suggested that firm size is positively related to diversification because larger firms are posited to have more resources on which to base diversified entry. The coefficient for firm sales is thus expected to be positive.

FGrowth$_i$ is measured as the compound annual growth rate of total sales for firm i between 1978 and 1981. It is derived from the firm revenue figures available in the Compustat database for 1978 and 1981.[11] Resource-based theorists generally contend that the higher a firm's growth rate, the more likely it will diversify. This occurs because high growth signifies a high rate of creation of new resources. Unless these new resources are created in precise proportions such that they can be reapplied to existing businesses, the firm will find itself with excess resources and will thus likely diversify to exploit them.[12] Thus, the coefficient for firm growth is expected to be positive.

FR&DS$_i$ – R&D intensity for firm i – is measured as the weighted average of the ratio of firm i's R&D expenditure to its total revenue for the years 1978–1981:[13]

$$\sum_{t=1978}^{1981} (\text{R\&D expenditure}_{it}) / \sum_{t=1978}^{1981} (\text{Revenue}_{it})$$

This measure was derived from the Compustat database for the years 1978–1981.[14] High R&D intensity is traditionally proposed by resource-based theorists to be a proxy for technological resources, which are generally considered to be shareable, rent-accruing resources. As such, resource-based theory contends that high R&D intensity is likely to encourage and facilitate diversification. The coefficient for firm R&D intensity is thus expected to be positive.

FAdvS$_i$ – advertising intensity for firm i – is measured as the weighted average of the ratio of firm i's advertising expenditure to its total revenue for the years 1978–1981:[15]

$$\sum_{t=1978}^{1981} (\text{Advertising expenditure}_{it}) / \sum_{t=1978}^{1981} (\text{Revenue}_{it})$$

This measure was derived from the Compustat database for the years 1978–1981.[16] Much like R&D intensity, high advertising intensity is viewed as a proxy for rent-accruing firm-specific resources that are likely to be exploitable in multiple industries, and thus should facilitate corporate diversification. The coefficient for firm advertising intensity should therefore be positive.

Conventional firm–industry relatedness variables

DiffR&DS$_{ij}$ is defined as the absolute value of the difference between industry R&D intensity and firm R&D intensity: $| \text{IR\&DS}_j - \text{FR\&DS}_i |$. This measure is derived from the FTC Line of Business data and the Compustat data described above. The resource-based framework suggests that a firm will diversify into industries whose resource requirements are similar to its resource base. A large difference between firm and industry R&D intensity is traditionally posited to proxy for a large dissimilarity between firm i's technological resource base and industry j's technological resource requirements (see for example Montgomery and Hariharan 1991). The coefficient for the difference between firm i's and industry j's R&D intensities is therefore expected to be negative.

DiffAdvS$_{ij}$ is defined as the absolute value of the difference between industry advertising intensity and firm advertising intensity: | IAdvS$_j$ − FAdvS$_i$ |. This measure is derived from the FTC Line of Business data and the Compustat data described above. As was true for R&D intensity, the resource-based framework generally suggests that a large difference between firm and industry advertising intensity signifies a large dissimilarity between firm i's market-related resource base and industry j's market-related resource requirements. The coefficient for the difference between firm i's and industry j's advertising intensities is therefore expected to be negative.

Appropriability measures

Appropriability measures for innovation are derived from the Yale survey on research and development. In their survey of senior R&D executives at several hundred large US firms in the early 1980s, Levin *et al.* (1987) asked each respondent to rate on a seven-point Likert scale, for his/her specific line of business, the importance of the following mechanisms to appropriating returns to innovation: licensing royalties, secrecy, lead time, learning curve advantages, and control of sales and service.[17] This yielded industry-average ratings of the various appropriability mechanisms. Several scholars have used these to proxy for the overall strength of the appropriability regime in given industries, most frequently by taking the highest rating from across all six mechanisms (Levin *et al.* 1985; Cohen and Levinthal 1990). In this study I use them individually to proxy for industry-specific contracting hazards associated with exploiting innovation.

Royalty$_j$ is defined as the feasibility of licensing innovation in industry j. It is derived from the Yale survey by averaging all responses from industry j respondents to the question concerning the importance of royalties to exploiting innovations.[18] It is assumed that if license royalties are an effective mechanism for appropriating returns to innovation in industry j, then contracting for technology in industry j must be characterized by relatively low transaction costs. Hypothesis 2 proposes that, in such industries, firms will prefer to exploit their technological resources through contractual means rather than through expansion of their boundaries. Conversely, in industries where license royalties are not effective for appropriating returns, firms will have little alternative but to diversify if they are to exploit their technological resources. Thus, the coefficient for royalty importance is expected to be negative. A negative, significant coefficient for royalty importance will be interpreted as support for Hypothesis 2.[19]

Secrecy$_j$ is defined as the importance of secrecy to appropriating returns to innovation in industry j. It is derived from the Yale survey by averaging all responses from industry j respondents to the question concerning the importance of secrecy to exploiting innovations. It is assumed that in industries where secrecy is important, contracting for technology is subject to severe hazards, and diversification will be more prevalent. The coefficient for secrecy is therefore expected to be positive, and a positive significant coefficient will be interpreted as support for Hypothesis 2.

Learning$_j$ is defined as the importance of learning curve advantages to appropriating returns to innovation in industry j. It is derived from the Yale survey by averaging all responses from industry j respondents to the question concerning the importance of the learning curve to exploiting innovations. It is assumed that in industries where the learning curve is important, contracting for technology is difficult due to the necessity of transferring tacit knowledge, and diversification will be more prevalent.[20] The coefficient for learning curve is therefore expected to be positive, and a positive significant coefficient will be interpreted as support for Hypothesis 2.

Descriptive statistics

Table 5.2 presents the mean, standard deviation, minimum value and maximum value of each variable. In light of the suspected non-normal distribution of several of these variables, the exhibit also provides first quartile, median, and third quartile values. As described above, the sample constructed for my econometric estimation consists of all 1023 entries and a sample of 1491 non-entries between 1981 and 1985. Thus, while entry occurred in less than 0.5 percent of all potential entries in the general population under study, it occurred in slightly more than 40 percent of the cases included in this sample, as demonstrated by the mean of 0.407 for the Entry variable. Note that ISales (industry sales in $ billion) varies from a minimum of 0.067 to a maximum of 207.555, underscoring the great difference in the portion of the economy that is encompassed by different four-digit SIC codes. It is also worth pointing out that FGrowth (compound annual growth rate for firms) has a minimum value of -38.728 percent, which was experienced by the unfortunate Sunshine Mining Company. The values for WgtAbsTech, UnwgtAbsTech, WgtRelTech, and UnwgtRelTech all have means that are much closer to 0 than to their maximum values, and very large standard deviations relative to their means, which underscores the fact that there are many instances in which a firm has no technological resources (as measured by patents) that are applicable to a particular industry. The skewed distribution of these variables is further underscored by comparison of mean to median and quartile values: for all technology applicability variables (as well as for industry sales and firm sales), the means exceed third quartile values.

Table 5.3 presents the correlation matrix among the independent variables,

Table 5.2 Descriptive statistics of the independent variables

Variable (units)	Mean	Std. Dev.	Minimum	Maximum	Quartile 1	Median	Quartile 3
Entry (0–1)[a]	0.407	0.491	0.000	1.000	0.000	1.000	1.000
ISales ($B)[a]	5.502	13.078	0.067	207.555	1.174	2.610	5.297
IGrowth (%)[a]	10.011	6.084	−10.440	87.630	7.280	9.640	12.845
IConc (%)[a]	37.465	20.715	3.000	99.000	22.000	35.000	50.000
IR&DS (%)[a]	1.662	1.948	0.000	10.920	0.430	1.060	2.090
IAdvS (%)[a]	1.555	2.313	0.010	19.500	0.380	0.700	1.590
FSales ($B)[a]	3.737	10.710	0.008	65.564	0.268	1.000	3.450
FGrowth (%)[a]	4.191	11.116	−38.728	63.027	−2.093	2.806	9.717
FR&DS (%)[a]	1.762	1.756	0.000	9.912	0.546	1.184	2.376
FAdvS (%)[a]	1.227	2.410	0.000	15.642	0.000	0.175	1.309
DiffR&D (%)[a]	1.665	1.835	0.000	10.920	0.438	1.020	2.145
DiffAdv (%)[a]	1.860	2.655	0.003	19.500	0.380	0.810	2.050
WgtAbsTech (pats)[a]	3.020	19.259	0.000	489.132	0.002	0.051	0.630
WgtRelTech (pats)[a]	0.038	0.107	0.000	1.000	0.0002	0.003	0.022
UnwgtAbsTech (pats)[a]	3.050	15.593	0.000	428.734	0.002	0.070	0.786
UnwgtRelTech (pats)[a]	0.052	0.120	0.000	1.000	0.0004	0.005	0.040
Royalty (7-pt scale)[b]	3.134	1.157	1.000	7.000	2.165	3.165	3.940
Secrecy (7-pt scale)[b]	3.639	1.008	0.665	6.500	3.000	3.750	4.175
Learning (7-pt scale)[b]	5.054	0.779	2.000	7.000	4.625	5.085	5.500

Notes
a n = 2514
b n = 1380.

Table 5.3 Correlation matrix of the independent variables (excluding appropriability variables) (n = 2514)

Variable	ISales	IGrowth	IConc	IR&DS	IAdvS	FSales	FGrowth	FR&DS	FAdvS	Diff R&D	Diff Adv	WgtAbs Tech	WgtRel Tech	Unwgt AbsTech
IGrowth	0.170													
IConc	-0.031	-0.046												
IR&DS	0.110	0.344	0.173											
IAdvS	-0.070	-0.080	0.132	-0.008										
FSales	0.004	0.043	0.009	0.024	-0.018									
FGrowth	0.017	0.025	0.020	0.016	-0.028	0.052								
FR&DS	0.008	0.062	0.020	0.110	0.003	0.008	0.149							
FAdvs	-0.028	-0.011	0.006	-0.004	0.068	-0.063	0.010	0.105						
DiffR&D	0.092	0.172	0.077	0.531	0.016	0.013	0.123	0.010	0.539					
DiffAdv	-0.050	-0.045	0.082	-0.029	0.664	-0.049	0.002	0.049	0.002	0.014				
WgtAbsTech	0.096	0.087	-0.003	0.136	-0.019	0.158	-0.000	0.113	0.601	0.018	-0.033			
WgtRelTech	0.249	0.115	-0.095	0.198	-0.063	-0.011	0.039	-0.017	-0.033	0.033	-0.060	0.320		
UnwgtAbsTech	0.052	0.086	0.012	0.137	-0.039	0.218	0.002	0.113	-0.014	0.001	-0.060	0.812	0.245	
UnwgtRelTech	0.152	0.112	-0.056	0.246	-0.069	0.017	0.053	0.031	-0.043	0.020	-0.075	0.358	0.823	0.405

Note
$|p| > 0.039$ is significant at the 95% level. $|p| > 0.051$ is significant at the 99% level.

Table 5.4 Correlation matrix for the appropriability variables (n = 1380)

Variable	Royalty	Secrecy	Learning
Royalty			
Secrecy	0.003		
Learning	0.154	0.161	
ISales	0.107	0.002	−0.020
IGrowth	−0.099	−0.029	0.108
IConc	0.128	0.155	0.023
IR&DS	−0.147	0.049	0.110
IAdvS	−0.095	0.151	−0.048
FSales	0.024	−0.060	0.019
FGrowth	0.003	0.030	0.033
FR&DS	−0.029	−0.015	0.006
FAdvS	0.005	−0.015	−0.022
DiffR&D	−0.127	−0.001	0.066
DiffAdv	−0.057	0.088	−0.059
WgtAbsTech	−0.027	−0.030	0.016
WgtRelTech	−0.017	0.017	0.032
UnwgtAbsTech	−0.003	−0.033	0.022
UnwgtRelTech	−0.009	0.009	0.013

Note
| p | > 0.053 is significant at the 95% level. | p | > 0.069 is significant at the 99% level.

excluding the appropriability variables. Table 5.4 presents the correlation matrix for the appropriability variables. As expected, there is a very high correlation between weighted and unweighted measures of technological applicability, WgtAbsTech and UnwgtAbsTech (and between WgtRelTech and UnwgtRelTech). Also unsurprisingly, IR&DS and DiffR&D are highly correlated. This is to be expected because the expected value of DiffR&D conditional on an extreme industry R&D intensity is higher than the expected value conditional on an industry R&D intensity close to the mean. Similarly, high correlations exist between IAdvS and DiffAdv, between FR&DS and DiffR&D, and between FAdvS and DiffAdv. More surprising is the lack of negative correlation between Royalty on the one hand and Secrecy and Learning on the other.

Logit estimation: results and discussion

The phenomenon under study in this thesis is best described by a categorical variable – either entry takes place or it does not. There are several functional forms that can be used to model this process, the most common of which are logit and probit. In many studies, either logit or probit can be used, and selection is a matter of taste.[21] However, because my data set comes from state-based sampling, probit is not appropriate. Manski and McFadden (1981) have demonstrated that logit estimation using data derived from state-based sampling will yield unbiased and consistent coefficients for all variables except for the constant term.[22] The same is not true for probit. I therefore used a logit in this study.

Effect of technological applicability measures

The first set of logit estimates are presented in Table 5.5. The results for the regression using only traditional measures of entry barriers and firm-specific resources (model 1) are generally consistent with those of previous studies. All variables are signed as expected. All variables except for IAdvS and IGrowth are significant at the 99 percent level, and IAdvS, about whose effect there were conflicting expectations, is significant at the 95 percent level. The only surprise of this regression is the lack of significance of industry growth, which is commonly considered to be one of the primary influences on entry. Nevertheless, there is some empirical precedent for this finding. Montgomery and Hariharan (1991) and Lemelin (1982) both found destination industry growth to be an erratic predictor of diversifying entry, frequently insignificant and sensitive to measurement sources. Further, it is possible that the timing of my study – which includes the 1981–1982 recession – might distort the effect of industry growth on entry.

Addition of my measures of technological resource applicability to the model produces striking results. All four measures of technological applicability – sales-weighted absolute (models 2 and 4), sales-weighted relative (models 3 and 4), unweighted absolute (models 5 and 7), and unweighted relative (models 6 and 7) – are signed in the expected direction and significant at the 99 percent level. Further, the log-likelihood ratio test demonstrates that the technological similarity measures significantly improve the fit of the model: the critical value for the chi-square distribution at a 99 percent confidence level is 6.64, and the likelihood ratios for models 2 through 7 as compared to model 1 are all 90.60 or greater. Thus I can reject the null hypothesis that addition of the technological applicability measures does not improve the explanatory power of my model. These results support Hypothesis 1. At the same time, the coefficients for the conventional model's variables largely retain the same magnitudes and levels of significance.

The results of models 4 and 7 suggest that a firm's diversification pattern is influenced by both the relative and the absolute levels of its technological resources. When both measures are included in a single model, their coefficients remain positive and significant. The model is able to discern these separate effects despite the moderate correlation between absolute and relative technological applicability. Further, inclusion of both measures significantly increases the explanatory power of the model according to the likelihood ratio test.

While the impact of technological applicability is robust across all specifications in Table 5.5, model 4, which includes both WgtAbsTech and WgtRelTech, provides the best fit. Figure 5.5 shows the improvement in prediction

Model (1): Conventional resource-based model
(constant; firm variables; industry variables; conventional measures of relationship between firm resources and industry resource needs)

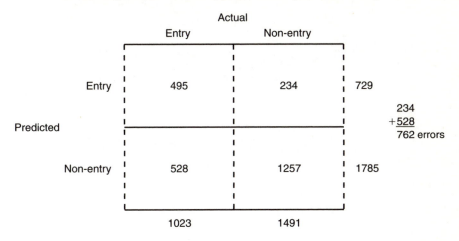

Model (4): New technological resource model
(Model 1 variable plus WgtAbsTech and WgtRelTech)

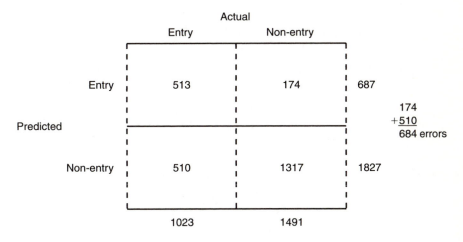

Figure 5.5 Predicted vs. actual entry.

afforded by model 4 over model 1. Where the conventional model makes 762 errors in prediction of entry for the sample data, identification of specific technological resources and their likely industries of applicability cuts this error rate by 10 percent to 684 errors.[23] Model 4 is used as the baseline for subsequent empirical tests throughout the rest of this chapter.

Table 5.5 Logit estimation of entry: technological applicability measures (n = 2514; standard errors in parentheses; ** = p < 0.01, * = p < 0.05)

	(1)	(2)	(3)	(4)	(5)	(6)	(7)
Intercept	-0.276*	-0.263	-0.443**	-0.377**	-0.220	-0.435**	-0.347**
	(0.132)	(0.135)	(0.135)	(0.137)	(0.135)	(0.135)	(0.137)
ISales	0.017**	0.010**	0.008*	0.007	0.010**	0.010**	0.010**
	(0.005)	(0.004)	(0.003)	(0.004)	(0.004)	(0.004)	(0.003)
IGrowth	0.010	0.006	0.009	0.007	0.006	0.009	0.007
	(0.007)	(0.008)	(0.008)	(0.008)	(0.008)	(0.008)	(0.008)
IConc	-0.024**	-0.022**	-0.021**	-0.021**	-0.024**	-0.022**	-0.023**
	(0.002)	(0.002)	(0.002)	(0.003)	(0.002)	(0.002)	(0.003)
IR&DS	0.567**	0.470**	0.500**	0.454**	0.481**	0.476**	0.448**
	(0.039)	(0.039)	(0.039)	(0.039)	(0.040)	(0.039)	(0.040)
IAdvS	0.076*	0.066*	0.071*	0.065*	0.069*	0.073*	0.069*
	(0.032)	(0.032)	(0.032)	(0.032)	(0.032)	(0.032)	(0.033)
FSales	0.033**	0.020**	0.030**	0.020**	0.020**	0.030**	0.020**
	(0.006)	(0.006)	(0.006)	(0.006)	(0.006)	(0.006)	(0.006)
FGrowth	0.016**	0.017**	0.014**	0.016**	0.017**	0.014**	0.015**
	(0.004)	(0.004)	(0.004)	(0.004)	(0.004)	(0.004)	(0.004)
FR&DS	0.152**	0.059	0.147**	0.082*	0.061	0.121**	0.070
	(0.036)	(0.037)	(0.037)	(0.038)	(0.037)	(0.037)	(0.038)
FAdvS	0.113**	0.122**	0.107**	0.117**	0.120**	0.104**	0.112**
	(0.029)	(0.030)	(0.029)	(0.030)	(0.030)	(0.029)	(0.030)
DiffR&D	-0.467**	-0.381**	-0.427**	-0.379**	-0.379**	-0.398**	-0.361**
	(0.043)	(0.044)	(0.043)	(0.044)	(0.044)	(0.044)	(0.044)
DiffAdv	-0.180**	-0.170**	-0.169**	-0.167**	-0.170**	-0.162**	-0.162**
	(0.035)	(0.036)	(0.036)	(0.036)	(0.036)	(0.036)	(0.036)

	Model 1	Model 2	Model 3	Model 4	Model 5	Model 6	Model 7
WgtAbsTech		0.185** (0.035)		0.134** (0.024)			
WgtRelTech			6.076** (0.796)	3.700** (0.776)			
UnwgtAbsTech					0.118** (0.019)		0.079** (0.018)
UnwgtRelTech						4.863** (0.605)	3.248** (0.628)
Log-lklhd	−1443.66	−1381.85	−1397.51	−1366.69	−1396.81	−1398.36	−1380.54
Lklhd ratio test		$\chi^2(1)$ vs. model 1 = 134.2**	$\chi^2(1)$ vs. model 2 = 35.5**				
No. of correct predictions	1752	1820	1809	1830	1792	1800	1819

Effect on estimated probabilities

The above section has described the sign and significance of parameters in my models, but has not explored the direct effect of technological resource applicability or of conventional variables on the estimated probability of entry. Logit estimation does not yield coefficients that can be directly interpreted as probabilities. Since logit is not a linear form, the effect of a change in an independent variable varies depending on the initial level of that variable (and depending on the value of the other variables in the model). Specifically, to determine the effect on the probability of entry of a change in an independent variable from x to x', one must calculate:

$$\frac{\exp\{\beta X'\}}{[1 + \exp\{\beta X'\}]} - \frac{\exp\{\beta X\}}{[1 + \exp\{\beta X\}]}$$

where X and X' are vectors of all independent variables in the model and X' differs from X only in that the variable of concern equals x' rather than x. Table 5.6 shows the effect on the estimated probability of diversifying entry of an increase in each independent variable from its mean to one standard deviation above the mean, conditional on all other variables being at their mean values. Thus, for an observation with mean values for all other variables, such an increase in the absolute applicability of firm i's technological resource base to industry j ($WgtAbsTech_{ij}$) would increase the probability that firm i diversifies

Table 5.6 Changes in estimated probabilities of entry (effect of changing independent variable from mean value to 1 standard deviation above the mean) (1)

Variable (units)	Mean	1 std. dev. above mean	P(entry | var. at 1 std. dev. above mean)[a]	Change from P(entry | var. at mean)[a]	Rank in importance
ISales ($B)	5.502	18.580	0.479	+0.023	12
IGrowth (%)	10.011	16.095	0.467	+0.011	13
IConc (%)	37.465	58.180	0.352	−0.104	5
IR&DS (%)	1.662	3.610	0.667	+0.214	2
IAdvS (%)	1.555	3.868	0.493	+0.037	10
FSales ($B)	3.737	14.447	0.501	+0.045	8
Growth (%)	4.191	15.307	0.500	+0.044	9
FR&DS (%)	1.762	3.518	0.492	+0.036	11
FAdvs (%)	1.227	3.637	0.526	+0.070	7
DiffR&D (%)	1.665	3.500	0.295	−0.161	3
Diffadv (%)	1.860	4.515	0.350	−0.106	4
WgtAbsTech (patents)	3.020	22.279	0.917	+ 0.461	1
WgtRelTech (patents)	0.038	0.145	0.555	+ 0.099	6

Note
a Assuming all other variables are held constant at their mean values.

into industry j by 46.1 percent. To demonstrate the importance of technological resources another way, if WgtAbsTech$_{ij}$ is one standard deviation above the mean, then firm i is likely to diversify into industry j even if all of the industry variables are one standard deviation below their means[24] (Prob[Div$_{ij}$ = 1] = 69.2 percent) or if all of the firm variables are one standard deviation below their means (Prob[Div$_{ij}$ = 1] = 61.2 percent). The technological applicability variable has a larger impact on probability of entry than any other independent variable.[25]

How important are the various sets of variables to potential entry? Changing the entire set of industry variables – ISales, IGrowth, IConc, IR&DS, and IAdvS – simultaneously to one standard deviation above their mean values increases the probability of entry by 35 percent, to slightly more than 80 percent.[26] By comparison, shifting the set of firm variables – FSales, FGrowth, FR&DS and FAdvS – to one standard deviation above their means yields an increase in the probability of entry of just under 20 percent, to approximately 65 percent. Thus, industry characteristics appear to wield greater influence over the probability of entry than do firm characteristics. This result, however, should not be taken as evidence that entry barrier theory (which is industry-based) better explains entry than firm effects. In fact, traditional entry barrier theory proposes that industry R&D intensity and industry advertising intensity should deter entry. In contrast, this study anticipated and found that these industry characteristics encourage entry (as did Montgomery and Hariharan 1991). To see the effect of reducing entry barriers on entry, we must decrease IR&DS and IAdvS to one standard deviation below their mean values (as well as decreasing IConc and increasing IGrowth by one standard deviation).[27] The effect of reducing entry barriers (as stipulated by traditional entry barrier theory) by one standard deviation from the mean is to *reduce* the probability of entry by 7 percent. Thus, my results suggest that the probability of entry is not influenced by entry barriers (at least not in the traditional direction), is heavily influenced by the set of firm factors traditionally hypothesized by resource-based theorists as important, and is most heavily influenced by the set of firm–industry relatedness characteristics that form the heart of the resource-based approach.

As Table 5.2 showed, however, several independent variables in my model have skewed distributions. Table 5.7 recalculates the changes in estimated probability of entry using median and quartile figures as the parameters. Overall, the change in probability generated by each variable tends to be much lower than its counterpart in Table 5.6. This is to be expected because the median–quartile spreads are smaller than the mean–standard deviation spreads for these variables. A somewhat different picture emerges from Table 5.7, in which the effect of my technological resource measures are significantly reduced both in size and in importance relative to other independent variables. The relative importance of entry barrier variables, industry variables, firm variables, and firm–industry relatedness variables remains the same.

Table 5.7 Changes in estimated probabilities of entry (effect of changing independent variable from median value to third quartile value) (2)

Variable (units)	Median	Third quartile	P(entry | var.at third quartile)[a]	Change from P(entry | var. at median)[a]	Rank in importance
ISales ($B)	2.610	5.297	0.460	+0.004	13
IGrowth (%)	9.640	12.845	0.461	+0.005	12
IConc (%)	35.000	50.000	0.394	−0.062	3
IR&DS (%)	1.060	2.090	0.569	+0.113	1
IAdvS (%)	0.700	1.590	0.468	+0.012	10
FSales ($B)	1.010	3.450	0.466	+0.010	11
Growth (%)	2.806	9.717	0.480	+0.024	5
FR&DS (%)	1.184	2.376	0.477	+0.021	7
FAdvs (%)	0.175	1.309	0.485	+0.029	6
DiffR&D (%)	1.020	2.145	0.375	−0.081	2
Diffadv (%)	0.810	2.050	0.414	−0.042	4
WgtAbsTech (patents)	0.051	0.630	0.473	+0.017	8
WgtRelTech (patents)	0.003	0.022	0.472	+0.016	9

Note
a Assuming all other variables are held constant at their median values.

Effect of appropriability measures

The second set of logit estimations are presented in Table 5.8. As described above, measures of appropriability – importance of royalties, secrecy, and the learning curve – are derived from the Yale survey on R&D. This survey covered only about half of the manufacturing SICs. Therefore, empirical tests involving these measures were restricted to the 621 entries and 759 non-entries in my sample for which Yale survey data was available. Models 1 and 4 in Table 5.8 recreate the conventional resource-based model and the model incorporating WgtAbsTech and WgtRelTech for the reduced sample. Comparison with Table 5.5 indicates that the results for the selected sample are substantially similar to those for the unconstrained sample.[28]

Addition of the appropriability measures yields modest support for the transaction cost hypothesis (H2). As expected, Royalty's coefficient is negatively signed, suggesting that a firm is less likely to diversify to exploit its technological resources when viable contractual alternatives exist. In addition, the coefficients for Secrecy and Learning curve are positively signed, implying that a firm is more likely to exploit its technological resources through diversification when those assets are either (1) subject to contracting hazards due to expropriation risks associated with information revelation or (2) characterized by cumulative, tacit knowledge, making their market transfer difficult. On a less encouraging note, Secrecy does not have a significant effect on diversification in any specification, and Royalty has a significant effect only in conjunction with the other appropriability variables. Nevertheless, I interpret the results of

Table 5.8 Logit estimation of entry: appropriability regime effects (n = 1380; standard errors in parentheses; ** = p < 0.01; * = p < 0.05)

	(1)[a]	(4)[a]	(8)	(9)	(10)	(11)
Intercept	−0.215	−0.322	−0.010	−0.629*	−1.156*	−1.087*
	(0.180)	(0.187)	(0.254)	(0.290)	(0.458)	(0.495)
ISales	0.011**	0.005	0.006	0.005	0.005	0.006
	(0.004)	(0.004)	(0.004)	(0.004)	(0.004)	(0.004)
IGrowth	−0.004	−0.004	−0.005	−0.003	−0.005	−0.006
	(0.010)	(0.010)	(0.010)	(0.010)	(0.010)	(0.011)
IConc	−0.021**	−0.019**	−0.018**	−0.019**	−0.019**	−0.019**
	(0.003)	(0.003)	(0.003)	(0.003)	(0.003)	(0.003)
IR&DS	0.582**	0.480**	0.477**	0.480**	0.478**	0.471**
	(0.050)	(0.050)	(0.050)	(0.050)	(0.050)	(0.051)
IAdvS	0.120*	0.115*	0.110*	0.110*	0.115*	0.106*
	(0.046)	(0.047)	(0.047)	(0.047)	(0.047)	(0.047)
FSales	0.057**	0.035**	0.035**	0.036**	0.036**	0.037**
	(0.013)	(0.012)	(0.012)	(0.012)	(0.012)	(0.012)
FGrowth	0.019**	0.017**	0.017**	0.017**	0.017**	0.017**
	(0.006)	(0.006)	(0.006)	(0.006)	(0.006)	(0.006)
FR&DS	0.140**	0.083	0.086	0.083	0.086	0.091
	(0.048)	(0.049)	(0.049)	(0.049)	(0.049)	(0.049)
FAdvS	0.107*	0.127**	0.129**	0.128**	0.123**	0.126**
	(0.044)	(0.045)	(0.046)	(0.045)	(0.045)	(0.046)
DiffR&D	−0.460**	−0.379**	−0.385**	−0.377**	−0.378**	−0.386**
	(0.056)	(0.057)	(0.057)	(0.057)	(0.057)	(0.057)
DiffAdv	−0.212**	−0.215**	−0.217**	−0.215**	−0.211**	−0.213**
	(0.053)	(0.054)	(0.054)	(0.054)	(0.054)	(0.054)
WgtAbsTech		0.131**	0.129**	0.129**	0.128**	0.126**
		(0.031)	(0.031)	(0.031)	(0.031)	(0.031)
WgtRelTech		3.004**	2.991**	2.973**	3.011**	2.973**
		(0.862)	(0.862)	(0.860)	(0.864)	(0.862)
Royalty			−0.051			−0.062*
			(0.028)			(0.029)
Secrecy				0.045		4.863**
				(0.033)		(0.605)
Learning					0.084*	0.093*
					(0.042)	(0.044)
Log-lklhd	−791.14	−746.84	−745.16	−745.87	−744.81	−741.89
No. of correct predictions	963	1004	1009	1003	1005	1016

Note
a Reiteration of Model 1 and 4 from Table 5.5, including only observations for which appropriability data is available

model 11 as a rejection of the null hypothesis that variance in the contractual hazards attendant upon a resource has no effect on diversification behavior, and thus as modest support for Hypothesis 2.[29] I also consider the existence of results consonant with the transaction cost hypothesis even within a single class of resource evidence that, across the range of rent-producing resources, transaction cost logic must be explicitly incorporated.

Industry of manufacture vs. industry of use

As described in Chapter 4, a patent can be assigned to either a SIC of Manufacture or a SIC of Use. Thus far in this chapter I have lumped both assignments together, implicitly assuming that a firm is as likely to exploit its technological resources by entering an industry where it can manufacture its patented technology as it is by entering an industry where it can use its technology. It is possible that one of these technology exploitation routes dominates corporate diversification behavior – that firms almost always enter the business in which their technology can be used rather than where it can be manufactured (or vice versa).

To test this, I re-ran estimation of my model with the patent portfolio assignment by SIC of Use and SIC of Manufacture split into separate variables. Results appear in Table 5.9. The baseline technological applicability model, model 4 from Table 5.5, is presented again for convenience. Models 12 and 13 replace the baseline technological measures with measures derived strictly from assignments to industries of use (WgtAbsTechUse, WgtRelTechUse) and industries of manufacture (WgtAbsTechMfre, WgtRelTechMfre), respectively. All of these measures are of similar levels of magnitude and significance. Model 14 includes both use- and manufacture-oriented technological applicability measures, thus allowing for differential effects on diversification of technological resources based on use and on manufacture. Using the likelihood ratio test, I cannot reject the null hypothesis that the baseline model offers as much predictive power as model 14.

While neither use nor manufacture information provides an improved fit across all industries, it is possible that for certain subsets of industries or technologies these will provide better fits. Pavitt (1984) and Pavitt *et al.* (1989) typologize industries by their primary source(s) of technological innovation. "Supplier-dominated" industries are those that derive most of their innovations from upstream suppliers. These authors postulate that supplier-dominated industries are vulnerable to forward integration by upstream firms able to exploit their relevant technological skills. Conversely, other industries are characterized by the need for user input to the innovation process. These industries are vulnerable to technology-driven backward integration. (For somewhat obscure reasons, Pavitt *et al.* categorize this latter set of industries as "specialized supplier" industries. I will term them "user-dominated" industries for clarity.)

What would the Pavitt conjecture mean for my estimation? If it is true that supplier-dominated industries are prey to forward integration by technologically advanced suppliers, then for such industries one would expect entry to be more strongly driven by SIC of Use than by SIC of Manufacture. If user-dominated industries face a strong threat of backward integration by these users, then for such industries entry should be driven primarily by SIC of Manufacture rather than by SIC of Use. Using these two categories from the Pavitt *et al.* typology, I test this empirically.

The Yale survey asked respondents to rate the importance of several sources of

Table 5.9 Logit estimation of entry: industry of use vs. industry of manufacture (n = 2514; standard errors in parentheses; ** = p < 0.01; * = p < 0.05)

	(4)	(12)	(13)	(14)
Intercept	−0.377**	−0.347**	−0.366**	−0.375**
	(0.137)	(0.136)	(0.137)	(0.137)
ISales	0.007	0.006	0.008	0.007
	(0.004)	(0.004)	(0.004)	(0.004)
IGrowth	0.007	0.009	0.005	0.007
	(0.008)	(0.008)	(0.008)	(0.008)
IConc	−0.021**	−0.022**	−0.021**	−0.021**
	(0.002)	(0.002)	(0.003)	(0.003)
IR&DS	0.454**	0.470**	0.460**	0.453**
	(0.039)	(0.039)	(0.039)	(0.039)
IAdvS	0.065*	0.067*	0.067*	0.065*
	(0.032)	(0.033)	(0.033)	(0.033)
FSales	0.020**	0.020**	0.020**	0.020**
	(0.006)	(0.006)	(0.006)	(0.006)
FGrowth	0.016**	0.017**	0.015**	0.016**
	(0.004)	(0.004)	(0.004)	(0.004)
FR&DS	0.082*	0.093*	0.079*	0.082*
	(0.038)	(0.038)	(0.038)	(0.038)
FAdvS	0.117**	0.113**	0.120**	0.115**
	(0.030)	(0.030)	(0.030)	(0.030)
DiffR&D	−0.379**	−0.393**	−0.381**	−0.379**
	(0.044)	(0.044)	(0.044)	(0.044)
DiffAdv	−0.167**	−0.166**	−0.171**	−0.166**
	(0.036)	(0.036)	(0.036)	(0.036)
WgtAbsTech	0.134**			
	(0.024)			
WgtRelTech	3.700**			
	(0.776)			
WgtAbsTechUse		0.296**		0.097
		(0.059)		(0.073)
WgtRelTechUse		3.750**		2.512**
		(0.839)		(1.048)
WgtAbsTechMfre			0.217**	0.159**
			(0.039)	(0.052)
WgtRelTechMfre			2.577**	1.378**
			(0.614)	(0.773)
Log-lklhd	−1366.69	−1377.28	−1372.82	−1366.41
No. of correct predictions	1830	1828	1823	1833

innovation in their respective industries, including material suppliers, equipment suppliers, and users.[30] I categorized those industries for which the importance of material suppliers or equipment suppliers as sources of innovation was rated above the mean as supplier-dominated industries.[31] Those industries for which the importance of users as sources of innovation was rated above the mean were categorized as user-dominated industries. Industries with below-average ratings for the importance of suppliers and/or of users were categorized as non-supplier-dominated and non-user-dominated, respectively. I then ran separate estimations of models 4, 12, and 13 for these different industry categories.

Rather than present the entire estimation results, which remain substantially the same across all runs, Table 5.10 identifies which specification of technological resources – SIC of Use, SIC of Manufacture, or the baseline combination of both SICs – offers the best fit for each industry category, as measured by the log-likelihood ratio. As the table shows, the SIC of Manufacture measure provides the best fit for user-dominated industries. The SIC of Use measure provides the best fit for supplier-dominated industries. For industries that are neither user- nor supplier-dominated, the baseline model provides the best fit.

These results provide at least crude empirical support for the contention by Pavitt and his colleagues that the direction of technology-based entry varies across industries as the primary source of innovation varies.

Technology-intensive vs. technology-indifferent firms

Finally, I tested whether the significant influence of technological resources on diversification varied with the technological intensity of firms under examination. I divided the sample of firms in two different ways: (1) Jaffe vs. non-Jaffe firms (where, as before, Jaffe firms are considered to be technology-intensive and non-Jaffe firms are non-intensive); and (2) firms with patent portfolios of 50 or more patents vs. firms with patent portfolios of fewer than 50 patents and fewer than 20 patents.[32] As Table 5.11 shows, the technological applicability measures are significant and positive for the Jaffe firms and for the set of firms with large patent portfolios. For non-Jaffe firms and firms with small patent port-

Table 5.10 SIC of Use and SIC of Manufacture variables (as function of source of innovation)

Type of industry	N	Technological measures offering best fit[a]	Statistically significant improvement over next-best model?[b]
User-dominated	373 entries 399 non-entries	WgtAbsTechMfre; WgtRelTechMfre	Yes (99%)
Supplier-dominated (equipment suppliers)	300 entries 422 non-entries	WgtAbsTechUse; WgtRelTechUse	Yes (95%)
Supplier-dominated (materials suppliers)	356 entries 404 non-entries	WgtAbsTech; WgtRelTech	No
Non-dominated	181 entries 224 non-entries	WgtAbsTech; WgtRelTech	No

Notes
a As measured by log-likelihood.
b As measured by likelihood ratio test.
The numbers in the above table do not sum to the sample N of 2514 because some industries are dominated by more than one source of innovation.

Table 5.11 Logit estimation of entry: technology-intensive vs. non-intensive firms (standard errors in parentheses; ** = p < 0.01; * = p < 0.05)

	Non-intensive[a]	Technology intensive[a]	Number of patents in portfolio		
			<20	<50	> =50
Intercept	−0.919	−0.299	−0.434	−0.586**	0.060
	(0.630)	(0.145)	(0.281)	(0.220)	(0.191)
ISales	0.017	0.007	0.017*	0.016**	0.001
	(0.011)	(0.004)	(0.007)	(0.006)	(0.005)
IGrowth	−0.017	0.008	−0.018	−0.003	−0.005
	(0.030)	(0.009)	(0.019)	(0.014)	(0.010)
IConc	−0.039**	−0.020**	−0.034**	−0.031**	−0.017**
	(0.014)	(0.003)	(0.006)	(0.004)	(0.003)
IR&DS	0.422**	0.437**	0.694**	0.504**	0.416**
	(0.153)	(0.041)	(0.094)	(0.063)	(0.053)
IAdvS	0.095	0.060*	0.109*	0.135**	−0.075
	(0.100)	(0.036)	(0.054)	(0.045)	(0.051)
FSales	−0.381	0.015*	0.080	0.128**	0.006
	(0.424)	(0.006)	(0.054)	(0.040)	(0.005)
FGrowth	−0.003	0.027**	−0.001	0.003	0.032**
	(0.019)	(0.005)	(0.007)	(0.006)	(0.007)
FR&DS	−0.021	0.063	0.076	0.097	−0.024
	(0.136)	(0.042)	(0.074)	(0.055)	(0.058)
FAdvS	0.334**	0.101**	0.141**	0.144**	0.092*
	(0.107)	(0.034)	(0.049)	(0.041)	(0.047)
DiffR&D	−0.338*	−0.337**	−0.630**	−0.465**	−0.281**
	(0.169)	(0.047)	(0.104)	(0.071)	(0.060)
DiffAdv	−0.211	−0.166**	−0.141*	−0.162**	−0.141**
	(0.137)	(0.040)	(0.060)	(0.050)	(0.056)
WgtAbsTech	1.574	0.124**	0.181	0.728*	0.091**
	(0.990)	(0.023)	(0.165)	(0.316)	(0.022)
WgtRelTech	7.416	3.142**	1.859	1.532	5.036**
	(4.461)	(0.778)	(1.043)	(1.139)	(1.491)
No. of correct predictions/N	241/278	1592/2236	623/810	910/1192	930/1522

Note
a Technology-intensive firms are those that were drawn from the Jaffe (1986) study. Non-intensive firms are those that were drawn from Compustat and do not appear in the Jaffe sample.

folios, however, the technological applicability measures had an insignificant effect on diversification. While this result is not surprising – at the limit, a firm with no patents cannot be influenced by its patent portfolio – it is worth noting as a useful reminder that there are limits to the generalizability of this research.

Conclusion

This analysis is to the best of my knowledge the first attempt to examine the effects of firm-specific technological resources as measured by patent data on industry-specific diversification behavior. It is also the first study explicitly to examine the role of transaction costs on diversification in the context of a resource-based theory of the firm. The results suggest that a firm's technological resource base, as manifested in its corporate patent portfolio, significantly influences its diversification decisions. In particular, a firm elects to enter markets in which it can exploit its existing technological resources and in which those assets are likely to confer advantage. In addition, the firm's diversification decision was found to be influenced by the severity of hazards surrounding contractual alternatives to diversification.

6 An empirical analysis of the effect of technological resources on the mode of corporate diversification

Introduction

While the previous chapter examined the effect of technological resources on the direction of diversification, this chapter explores their influence on diversification mode. Chapter 2 noted the dearth of theoretical and empirical research concerning the determinants of the mode of diversification, and Chapter 3 presented a framework in which a firm's choice of entry mode is influenced by the composition of its existing resource base. This chapter explores the modal choice of diversifying firms by specifying hypothetical implications of the above framework. I then empirically examine these hypotheses with a variation on the empirical analysis used in Chapter 5. In the course of this examination, I note that all previous research on the mode of diversification has rested on an implicit, untested assumption about the diversification decision process – that a firm first decides to diversify and then, conditional on that decision, decides on the mode to pursue. I undertake an empirical test to determine the validity of this assumption. Since this test does not lead me to reject the implicit assumption of previous work, I then empirically test my modal hypotheses with a subset of the data sample – specifically, with the 1023 entry observations out of the sample's 2514 total observations.

Hypotheses

As described in Chapters 2 and 3, a firm can diversify through one of two modes: acquisition or internal expansion. There is a general, long-standing belief among business scholars that related diversification should be pursued through internal growth while unrelated diversification is more appropriately undertaken through acquisition (Ansoff 1965). However, the rationale for this belief has not been clearly stated, and empirical support is meager (Yip 1982; Chatterjee 1990).

Chapter 3 explains why we expect to see firms rely on internal expansion building when they pursue related diversification. If a firm's existing resources are highly applicable to the entered business, then (1) the firm needs to access fewer additional resources than if its existing resource pool is not applicable,

(2) the firm is likely to already have requisite in-house management skill to oversee startup,[1] and (3) there is a higher risk of redundancy of assets if the firm chooses to access the remaining resources through acquisition (Ansoff 1965; Chatterjee 1990). In this instance, a firm is likely to pursue diversification through internal expansion. Thus, if "related diversification" is explicitly defined as "diversification that requires resources of which the firm's existing pool is a large subset," then related diversification is likely to be pursued through internal expansion.

Chapter 3 further argues that in diversification that exploits existing resources, there is a higher need for integration of the new business into existing operations. As Hill *et al.* (1992) have argued, firms composed of related businesses must invest in high levels of interdivisional coordination to exploit shared resources fully. Argyres (1995) contends that this is particularly true for exploitation of technological competences. In contrast, firms composed of unrelated businesses require little interdivisional coordination. Internal expansion facilitates integration because it avoids post-acquisition control problems and culture clashes (Hennart and Park 1993). There is a wealth of academic (e.g., Ansoff *et al.* 1971) and trade press evidence to suggest that the assimilation of acquired companies is a difficult, uncertain process. Thus this argument suggests a second resource-based rationale for favoring internal growth in related diversification.

To summarize, internal expansion is favored over acquisition when the cost and time necessary to build required resources are lower than the cost to buy them, and when a high degree of integration between the new business and existing operations is needed. Both of these are likely to occur when the firm's existing resource pool is highly applicable to its new business. Thus, the range of resource applicability should be a major determinant of diversification mode.

H1: Ceteris paribus, *the greater the extent to which a firm possesses the technological resources required to compete in a business, the greater the likelihood that the firm will diversify through internal expansion rather than through acquisition.*

As I argued in Chapter 5, not all companies are highly influenced by technology. It is likely that the hypothesis derived above will hold more strongly for those firms that have significant investments in technological resources than for those whose competitive advantage does not rest on technological resources.

H2: Ceteris paribus, *a firm's pattern of diversification mode choice will be more highly influenced by its technological resources the greater the absolute level of its technological resources.*

Specification of the model – mode of diversification

The hypotheses enumerated above concerning the mode of diversification can be tested in a logit model of entry into new markets similar to the model of direction tested in Chapter 5. Our model of modal choice in diversification follows in the tradition of Yip (1982), which remains the most comprehensive empirical study of the subject to date. As did Yip, I look at the choice between diversification by acquisition and diversification by internal expansion as a function of industry characteristics, firm characteristics, and characteristics representing the level of relatedness between the firm and the industry.[2] Given my contention that extension of the resource-based framework requires the direct examination of definable resources and their potential businesses of application, I improve upon Yip's model by including direct measures of the applicability of firm i's technological base to destination industry j.[3] The resulting model appears in Table 6.1.

Data

The research methodology for testing the hypotheses outlined above relies on data nearly identical to that used in Chapter 5. As was described in that chapter, this data is drawn from eight databases and compiled for 412 large US firms and 429 four-digit SIC industries in 1981 and 1985 (see pp. 48–58 for a detailed description).

Table 6.1 Model of diversification behavior: mode of diversification

$$P(DivInt_{ij} = 1) = \beta_0 + \beta_1 IGrowth_j + \beta_2 IConc_j + \beta_3 IR\&DInt_j + \beta_4 IAdvInt_j$$
$$+ \beta_5 FSales_i + \beta_6 FGrowth_i + \beta_7 FR\&DInt_i + \beta_8 FAdvInt_i$$
$$+ \beta_9 DiffR\&D_{ij} + \beta_{10} DiffAdv_{ij}$$
$$+ \beta_{11} AbsTech_{ij} + \beta_{12} RelTech_{ij}$$
$$+ \beta_{13} Royalty_j + \beta_{14} Secrecy_J + \beta_{15} Learning_j + e_{ij}$$

where:

$P(DivInt_{ij} = 1)$	The probability that firm i will diversify into industry j by internal expansion
$IGrowth_j$ (%)	CAGR of sales in industry j between 1978 and 1981
$IConc_j$ (%)	Four-firm concentration ratio in industry j in 1982
$IR\&DInt_j$ (%)	Industry-wide ratio of R&D expenditure to revenue in 1977
$IAdvInt_j$ (%)	Industry-wide ratio of advertising expenditure to revenue in 1977
$FSales_i$ ($ billion)	Sales for firm i in 1981
$FGrowth_i$ (%)	CAGR of sales by firm i between 1978 and 1981
$FR\&DInt_i$ (%)	Weighted average of the ratio of R&D expenditure to revenue for firm i, 1978–1981
$FAdvInt_i$ (%)	Weighted average of the ratio of advertising expenditure to revenue for firm i in 1978–1981
$DiffR\&D_{ij}$	Absolute value of the difference between industry R&D intensity and firm R&D intensity
$DiffAdv_{ij}$	Absolute value of the difference between industry advertising intensity and firm advertising intensity
$AbsTech_{ij}$	A measure of the applicability of firm i's patent portfolio to industry j in absolute terms
$RelTech_{ij}$	A measure of the applicability of firm i's patent portfolio to industry j, relative to the applicability of firm i's patent portfolio to other industries

The dependent variable

The dependent variable, $DivInt_{ij}$, is derived from the AGSM/Trinet Large Establishment database (Trinet) and is coded as a categorical variable:

$DivInt_{ij} = 1$ if firm i enters industry j through internal expansion, 0 if through acquisition.

In addition to the data compiled for US establishments with 20 or more employees that was discussed in the previous chapter, Trinet also assigned a unique establishment identification number to each establishment in its database. This establishment code is permanently assigned to a given establishment, and does not change with alterations in the establishment's parentage.[4] This enabled me to identify the mode of entry for all 1023 diversification moves in my sample. For each entry by firm i into industry j, I identified those establishments owned by firm i in 1985 that contained operations in industry j. Using the establishment ID numbers, I then determined whether these establishments existed in 1981, and, if so, whether they were owned by firm i or by another firm. Entries that were located in establishments that (1) did not exist in 1981, or (2) existed and were owned by firm i in 1981, are considered to be internal expansions and are coded as 1. Entries that were located in establishments that (1) existed in 1981 and (2) were not owned by firm i in 1981 are considered to be acquisitions, and are coded as 0.[5] Internal expansions accounted for 546 of the entries in my sample, and acquisitions accounted for the remaining 477.

The independent variables

The independent variables were constructed much as they were in Chapter 5.

New operationalizations of technological resources

$WgtAbsTech_{ij}$ is defined as the absolute level of firm i's patent portfolio that is likely to be applicable to industry j. For this empirical test I constructed absolute technological applicability measures using both weighted and unweighted concordance values. As I found in Chapter 5, the weighted values provided a more accurate measure than the unweighted values; the empirical results shown in this chapter therefore provide the weighted measures only. If firm i's patent portfolio is highly applicable to industry j, then firm i is likely to have in-house most or all of the requisite technological skills for industry j. Diversification by internal expansion is therefore more feasible than if firm i's patent portfolio is not applicable to industry j. Further, to the extent that technological resources are shared, the management of technological resources by the new business is likely to affect the technology's value in existing operations, thus requiring greater integration. Diversification by internal expansion is therefore more desirable to avoid control problems. The coefficient for the applicability of firm i's patent portfolio to industry j (in absolute terms) is therefore expected to be positive.

$WgtRelTech_{ij}$ is defined as the applicability of firm i's patent portfolio to industry j, relative to the applicability of firm i's patent portfolio to other industries. As such, it represents an alternative measure of the extent to which firm i's technological resources may satisfy the requirements of industry j. The coefficient for relative technological applicability is expected to be positive.

Industry variables[6]

Industry variables are included as control variables because entry barrier theory (as propounded by Yip) argues that entry barriers differentially affect the costs of internal growth and acquisition. However, given the marginal and contradictory results found by Yip (1982) and Chatterjee (1990) and my own skepticism regarding entry barrier theory (based on the poor results for entry barrier variables in the previous chapter's analysis), I am agnostic concerning the significance of any of the industry variables.

$IGrowth_j$ is measured as the compound annual growth rate of total sales in SIC j between 1978 and 1981. The entry barrier framework suggests entry by internal expansion (which, unlike entry by acquisition, changes the number of competitors and overall capacity in the industry) is likely to spark fewer repercussions in the presence of higher industry growth. The coefficient for industry growth is therefore expected to be positive. However, given Chatterjee's (1990) finding of a negative relationship between industry growth and diversification by internal expansion, I have no a priori expectation concerning the coefficient for industry growth.

$IConc_j$ is measured as the four-firm concentration ratio for industry j in 1982.[7] As entry by acquisition is expected to elicit less incumbent reaction than entry by internal expansion, higher market concentration (which raises the likelihood of incumbent reaction) should favor acquisition. On the other hand, as Yip (1982) has pointed out, high market concentration is correlated with heightened government concerns regarding antitrust, which may have a chilling effect on acquisitions.[8] High concentration is also likely to be negatively correlated with the availability of potential acquirees in that industry. Given these conflicting effects of concentration, I have no a priori expectation concerning the coefficient for industry concentration.

$IR\&DS_j$ – R&D intensity for industry j – is measured as the industry-wide ratio of R&D expenditure to total revenue in 1976. While there may be conflicting effects of industry R&D intensity on the likelihood of entry, to the extent that R&D produces industry-specific knowledge, higher R&D intensity is likely to be associated with a greater likelihood of acquisition. I therefore expect the coefficient for industry R&D intensity to be negative, if it is significant at all.

$IAdvS_j$ – advertising intensity for industry j – is measured as the industry-wide ratio of advertising expenditure to total revenue in 1976. Yip (1982) and others have suggested that advertising is a less formidable barrier than R&D because advertising budgets can be quickly ratcheted upward (or cut). The coefficient for industry-wide advertising intensity is thus expected to be negative, if it is significant at all.

Firm variables

$FSales_i$ is defined as the total annual sales of firm i in $ billion in 1981. Prior work in this area, invoking capital market imperfections, has suggested that firm size may be negatively related to internal expansion because larger firms are posited to have more financial resources with which to make an acquisition. On the other hand, a larger firm should also have a wider pool of (non-financial) resources on which to base internal expansion.[9] I therefore have no a priori expectation about the coefficient for $FSales_i$.

$FGrowth_i$ is measured as the compound annual growth rate of total sales for firm i between 1978 and 1981. Penrose (1959) argued that a firm's rate of growth is constrained by the amount of time its managers can allocate to managing growth. Further, firms are likely to alternate between growth spurts and "plateaus," during which they assimilate their most recent growth.[10] Some scholars (e.g., Ansoff 1965) have argued that acquisition circumvents these constraints on growth, since acquisitions usually provide their own managers with relevant experience. Thus, the coefficient for firm growth is expected to be negative, since higher firm growth in the past favors growth by acquisition over growth by internal expansion in the present.

$FR\&DS_i$ – R&D intensity for firm i – is measured as the weighted average of the ratio of firm i's R&D expenditure to its total revenue for the years 1978–1981. High R&D intensity is likely to represent a greater in-house repository of the resources necessary to compete in a new technology-intensive business. A diversifying firm with a high R&D intensity is less likely to need to acquire technological resources externally. The coefficient for firm R&D intensity is thus expected to be positive.

$FAdvS_i$ – advertising intensity for firm i – is measured as the weighted average of the ratio of firm i's advertising expenditure to its total revenue for the years 1978–1981. Much like R&D intensity, high advertising intensity is viewed as a proxy for rent-accruing firm-specific resources that are likely to be exploitable in multiple industries, and thus should facilitate internal expansion. The coefficient for firm advertising intensity should therefore be positive.

Conventional firm–industry relatedness variables

$DiffR\&DS_{ij}$ is defined as the absolute value of the difference between industry R&D intensity and firm R&D intensity. This measure captures one dimension of relatedness between diversifying firm and entered industry. A large difference between firm and industry R&D intensity is traditionally posited to proxy for a large dissimilarity between firm i's technological resource base and industry j's technological resource requirements (e.g., Montgomery and Hariharan 1991), and hence for a low likelihood that firm i has in-house the requisite technological skills for industry j. A lack of requisite skills internal to the firm raises the difficulty of diversification by internal expansion and favors diversification by acquisition. The coefficient for the difference between firm i's and industry j's R&D intensities is therefore expected to be negative.

DiffAdvS$_{ij}$ is defined as the absolute value of the difference between industry advertising intensity and firm advertising intensity. As was true for R&D intensity, the resource-based framework generally suggests that a large difference between firm and industry advertising intensity signifies a large dissimilarity between firm i's in-house market-related resource base and industry j's market-related resource requirements. The coefficient for the difference between firm i's and industry j's advertising intensities is therefore expected to be negative.

Descriptive statistics

Table 6.2 presents the mean, standard deviation, minimum value, maximum value, median, first quartile value, and third quartile value of each variable. As mentioned above, internal expansion accounts for more than half (53.4 percent) of all entries. This is lower than the proportion of internal expansions in Yip's (1982) and Chatterjee's (1990) samples (which were both roughly 65 percent). The discrepancy is likely due to methodological differences in sample selection and determination of the mode of diversification.[11]

It is worth noting that the mean values for WgtAbsTech and WgtRelTech are both roughly twice what they were in the Chapter 5 sample, which included non-entries. This underscores the role that technological resource applicability plays in the decision to diversify into a particular industry. Similarly, DiffAdv and DiffR&D are both somewhat smaller than their counterparts in the Chapter 5 sample (20 percent and 1 percent smaller, respectively). These differences have implications for the likely results of my empirical tests. I have hypothesized that mode choice will be affected by the relatedness of a firm's resource pool to an industry's resource requirements. However, Chapter 5 demonstrated that resource relatedness also affects the decision whether or not to enter a given industry. Since the mode choice model as presented above is conditional on entry having taken place, and since entry occurs relatively infrequently when firm i and industry j have a low level of resource relatedness, my mode choice sample includes a somewhat truncated range of resource relatedness. This "filtering" suggests that my independent variables should have less explanatory power in the mode choice estimations than they did in the direction of entry estimations.

Table 6.3 divides the sample observations into acquisitions and internal expansions, and provides the means of the independent variables for these two groups. Simple difference of means calculations are also presented. Most of the differences between the two groups are in the expected direction. For example,

Table 6.2 Descriptive statistics of the independent variables (n = 1023)

Variable (units)	Mean	Std. Dev.	Minimum	Maximum	Quartile 1	Median	Quartile 3
DivInt (0–1)[a]	0.534	0.499	0.000	1.000	0.000	1.000	1.000
IGrowth (%)	11.104	5.345	−10.310	33.190	8.148	10.665	13.639
IConc (%)	33.817	19.642	3.000	99.000	19.000	31.000	43.000
IR&DS (%)	2.242	2.277	0.000	10.920	0.650	1.390	3.010
IAdvS (%)	1.315	2.151	0.010	19.500	0.320	0.630	1.060
FSales ($B)	5.458	13.789	0.016	65.564	0.598	1.833	4.899
FGrowth (%)	5.000	10.901	−38.734	58.220	−1.036	2.954	10.571
FR&DS (%)	1.743	1.629	0.000	9.912	0.566	1.199	2.376
FAdvS (%)	1.181	2.256	0.000	12.557	0.000	0.175	1.259
DiffR&D (%)	1.615	1.777	0.000	9.999	0.400	0.996	2.173
DiffAdv (%)	1.503	2.310	0.003	18.891	0.320	0.684	1.490
WgtAbsTech (pats)	6.790	29.701	0.000	489.132	0.059	0.476	3.150
WgtRelTech (pats)	0.072	0.145	0.000	1.000	0.002	0.016	0.069

Note
a 0 = acquisition; 1 = internal expansion.

Table 6.3 Difference of means by diversification mode (n = 1023) (** = p < 0.01; * = p < 0.05)

Variable (units)	Mean: internal expansion	Mean: acquisition	T-statistic of difference
IGrowth (%)	11.664	10.463	3.606**
IConc (%)	35.180	32.258	2.379**
IR&DS (%)	2.354	2.114	1.687
IAdvS (%)	1.083	1.581	−3.715**
FSales ($B)	6.204	4.604	1.854
FGrowth (%)	4.054	6.083	−2.981**
FR&DS (%)	2.077	1.362	7.177**
FAdvS (%)	0.997	1.391	−2.791**
DiffR&D (%)	1.755	1.454	2.713**
DiffAdv (%)	1.230	1.815	−4.071**
WgtAbsTech (pats)	8.988	4.275	2.539*
WgtRelTech (pats)	0.076	0.068	0.903

internal expansion entries are characterized by significantly more applicable technological resources than are acquisition entries. The greatest surprise presented in Table 6.3 is that internal expansions are characterized (on average) by a greater difference between firm and industry R&D intensity than are acquisitions.

Table 6.4 presents the correlation matrix among the independent variables. Unsurprisingly, IR&DS and FR&DS are more highly correlated than they were in the full sample (including non-entries) in Chapter 5. IR&DS and DiffR&D are also more highly correlated in this subsample. More surprising is the reduction in correlation between FR&DS and DiffR&D in this subsample.

Aside: is the above model correct?

The model presented in Table 6.1, like its predecessors in Yip (1982) and Chatterjee (1990), implicitly assumes that firms first decide whether or not to diversify (and which industry to enter) and then, having decided to enter industry j, select a mode by which to enter (see Figure 6.1a for a pictorial description of this process). These studies thus focus only on the modal decision for a sample of observations where entry takes place. However, it is not clear that managers' decisions regarding diversification conform to this assumption. It is possible that managers consider the modal alternatives when deciding whether or not to diversify (see Figure 6.1b). Alternatively, managers may select both the direction and mode of diversification simultaneously (Figure 6.1c). There has been no empirical research to date that examines the above assumption, let alone attempts to determine which model of the diversification mode selection process is most accurate.

I do not attempt a full-blown examination of the ideal specification of this model.[12] In this section, I undertake a weak empirical test that indirectly bears

Table 6.4 Correlation matrix of the independent variables (n = 1023)

Variable	IGrowth	IConc	IR&DS	IAdvS	FSales	FGrowth	FR&DS	FAdvS	Diff R&D	Diff Adv	WgtAbs Tech
IGrowth											
IConc	0.041										
IR&DS	0.523	0.260									
IAdvS	−0.092	0.087	−0.015								
FSales	0.039	0.056	0.001	−0.043							
FGrowth	0.046	0.046	0.011	−0.047	0.068						
FR&DS	0.261	0.071	0.313	−0.018	−0.022	0.153					
FAdvs	−0.033	−0.012	0.014	0.220	−0.092	−0.007	0.134				
DiffR&D	0.414	0.142	0.705	−0.033	0.018	0.022	0.333	−0.002			
DiffAdv	−0.073	0.009	−0.009	0.663	−0.076	−0.031	0.076	0.630	−0.017		
WgtAbsTech	0.108	0.039	0.123	−0.008	0.160	−0.016	0.186	−0.049	0.031	−0.023	
WgtRelTech	0.114	−0.076	0.153	−0.035	−0.059	0.049	0.015	−0.032	0.076	−0.035	0.316

Note
| p | > 0.062 is significant at the 95% level. | p | > 0.081 is significant at the 99% level.

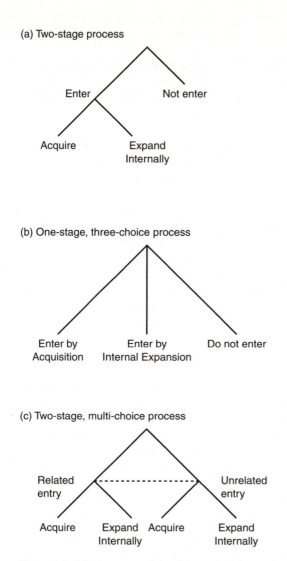

(a) Two-stage process

Enter   Not enter

Acquire   Expand
               Internally

(b) One-stage, three-choice process

Enter by   Enter by   Do not enter
Acquisition   Internal Expansion

(c) Two-stage, multi-choice process

Related <-------------------> Unrelated
entry   entry

Acquire   Expand Acquire   Expand
           Internally   Internally

Figure 6.1 Alternative models of diversification mode selection process.

on the validity of the traditional model. I can empirically test the model presented in Figure 6.1b with a multinomial logit specification and a trinary (rather than binary) dependent variable. I can then remove one of the dependent variable choices and employ the Hausman–McFadden specification test to check for the independence of irrelevant alternatives (IIA). If the true managerial decision process conforms to the model presented in Figure 6.1b, then I should find that the IIA assumption is not violated. Conversely, violation of IIA would indicate that this alternative model does not accurately depict reality.

Therefore, if I were to find in my empirical test that IIA is not violated, then the validity of the assumption implicit in the traditional model of modal choice would be highly suspect.[13]

For this test, I used the data as described above with two exceptions. First, all 2514 observations, rather than just the 1023 entry observations, were used in my estimation. Second, the dependent variable, DivMode$_{ij}$, was coded as a trinary categorical variable:

DivMode$_{ij}$ = 2 if firm i enters industry j through internal expansion,
             1 if firm i enters industry j through acquisition, and
             0 if firm i does not enter industry j.

To perform the Hausman–McFadden specification test, I ran two estimations. I first estimated the unconstrained model, which included both entry and non-entry observations and encompassed all three dependent variable categories. I then estimated a constrained model, in which I removed all non-entry observations. DivMode$_{ij}$ could thus only take on the values of 1 or 2 in the constrained estimation. The Hausman–McFadden specification test is performed by manipulating the coefficient vectors and the variance–covariance matrices of each estimation as follows:[14]

$$(\beta_u - \beta_c)'(\Sigma_c - \Sigma_u)^{-1}(\beta_u - \beta_c)$$

Where β_u equals the vector of coefficients from the unconstrained estimation, β_c equals the vector of coefficients from the constrained estimation, Σ_u equals the variance–covariance matrix from the unconstrained estimation, and Σ_c equals the variance–covariance matrix from the constrained estimation.[15]

This statistic is distributed chi-square, with degrees of freedom equal to the number of coefficients eliminated by the constrained model (in this case, 12). If this statistic is less than the value found in the chi-square table, then I cannot reject the IIA assumption. If it exceeds the value found in the chi-square table, then I can reject the assumption of IIA, which implies that the model under consideration is not accurate.

The test statistic derived from my empirical estimation is 200.01. The chi-square value associated with 12 degrees of freedom and a 95 percent confidence level is 25.25. I can therefore reject IIA, which leads me to reject the altern-ative model of diversification mode choice. For the rest of this chapter I will adhere to the model presented in Table 6.1, but it is important to reiterate that I have not demonstrated this model to be the best-fitting alternative. I have merely granted it a reprieve.

Logit estimation: results and discussion

Results of my logit estimations appear in Table 6.5. The results for my control variables, which relate to barriers to entry and to firm characteristics, are gener-

Table 6.5 Logit estimation of mode choice for diversifying entry (n = 1023; standard errors in parentheses; ** = p < 0.01; * = p < 0.05)

	Entire sample (1)	<50 patents (2)	50+ patents (3)
Intercept	−0.708**	−0.673	−0.804**
	(0.214)	(0.401)	(0.270)
IGrowth	0.034**	0.002	0.048**
	(0.015)	(0.030)	(0.018)
Iconc	0.011**	0.022**	0.006
	(0.004)	(0.008)	(0.004)
IR&DS	−0.146**	−0.053	−0.183**
	(0.052)	(0.088)	(0.068)
IadvS	−0.064	−0.229*	−0.009
	(0.048)	(0.095)	(0.065)
FSales	0.008	0.134	0.009*
	(0.005)	(0.075)	(0.005)
FGrowth	−0.025**	−0.008	−0.031**
	(0.006)	(0.012)	(0.008)
FR&DS	0.342**	0.178*	0.425**
	(0.052)	(0.085)	(0.071)
FAdvS	−0.057	−0.165	−0.004
	(0.044)	(0.090)	(0.060)
DiffR&D	0.082	0.149	0.067
	(0.060)	(0.108)	(0.077)
DiffAdv	−0.067	−0.048	−0.080
	(0.055)	(0.109)	(0.073)
WgtAbsTech	0.002	−0.030	−0.001
	(0.004)	(0.046)	(0.004)
WgtRelTech	0.592	−0.109	1.652*
	(0.507)	(0.820)	(0.763)
Log-lklhd	−651.198	−198.169	−435.491
No. of correct predictions/N	632/1023	197/327	452/696

ally consistent with prior research. Industry growth has a positive and significant coefficient, implying that entry by internal expansion is more attractive (or less discouraged) in industries experiencing rapid sales growth than in industries characterized by stagnant sales. The signs of the coefficients for industry R&D and advertising intensities are consonant with expectations; in addition, the significance of the former and insignificance of the latter conform to prior scholars' conjectures about their relative value as barriers to entry (see Yip 1982). All firm characteristics variables are signed as expected except for advertising intensity; while its coefficient is unexpectedly negative, it is insignificant. The one surprise among the control variables is industry concentration, which is positive and strongly significant. While there may be reasons to expect a positive relationship between concentration and internal expansion (as was described above, Yip conjectured that acquisition in highly concentrated industries might trigger antitrust concerns), prior empirical work has found that the negative effect of concentration outweighs the positive effect (Chatterjee 1990) or that the two effects negate each other (Yip 1982).

In model 1, which includes all entry observations, my measures of relatedness do not produce significant results. All but DiffR&D have the expected sign, but none of them is significant. In addition, a re-estimation of this model without the four relatedness variables yields a log-likelihood statistic of -653.955, which produces a likelihood ratio test statistic of 4.515.[16] Since the value for a chi-square distributed variable with several hundred observations, four degrees of freedom, and a 95 percent level of confidence is 9.488, I cannot reject the null hypothesis that my technological resource relatedness measures do not influence the mode of diversification.

Hypothesis 2 implies that technology-based relatedness, and particularly my new measures of patent portfolio applicability, will have a more pronounced effect on modal choice for technology-intensive diversifiers than for non-technology-intensive firms. I next divided my sample into two subsets: those observations that included firms whose patent portfolios consist of 50 or more patents (technology-intensive firms) and those whose portfolios contain fewer than 50 patents (non-technology-intensive). Models 2 and 3 present the results of estimations run separately on each subset. All of the control variables retain their signs in these estimations. It is worth noting, however, that industry R&D intensity loses its significance and industry advertising intensity becomes significant for the non-technology-intensive subset, as one would expect. The two technological applicability measures remain insignificant in this estimation. For the technology-intensive subset, the absolute measure of technological applicability remains insignificant. However, the relative measure of techno-logical applicability is positive and significant. Thus I cannot reject the null hypothesis that relative technological relatedness has no effect on mode choice. Estimations 2 and 3 provide support, albeit weak, for the hypothesis that technological applicability helps to inform diversifying firms' selection of entry mode. Further, the result of estimation 3 allows me to reframe my evaluation of Hypothesis 1. The results of my estimation on the full sample led me to reject Hypothesis 1, which stated that resource relatedness, and in particular techno-logical applicability, should influence mode choice in diversification. However, my subsequent test of Hypothesis 2 leads me to a weaker version of Hypothesis 1, which does receive modest support from model 3 in Table 6.5 (amendments underlined):

H1: Ceteris paribus, <u>for technology-intensive firms</u>, the greater the extent to which a firm possesses the <u>technological</u> resources required to compete in a business, the greater the likelihood that the firm will diversify through internal expansion rather than through acquisition.

Effect on estimated probabilities

The above section described the sign and significance (or lack thereof) of parameters in my model. This section examines the direct effect of technological resource relatedness on the estimated probability of mode choice. As described in Chapter 5, I calculate:

$$\frac{\exp\{\beta X'\}}{[1 + \exp\{\beta X'\}]} - \frac{\exp\{\beta X\}}{[1 + \exp\{\beta X\}]}$$

where X and X' are vectors of all independent variables in the model and X' differs from X only in that the variable of concern equals x' rather than x. Table 6.6 presents the effect on the estimated probability of diversifying by internal expansion of an increase in each independent variable from its mean to one standard deviation above the mean, with all other independent variables held constant at their mean values. Table 6.7 presents the effects of an increase in each independent variable from its median to its third quartile value. In each exhibit, two sets of probabilities are presented: one for the entire sample of entries and one for the subsample of entries by technology-intensive firms (those with patent portfolios of 50 or more patents). For the full sample, my relatedness variables, and particularly my technological applicability variables, have among the weakest effects on estimated probability of mode choice. However, for the technology-intensive subsample, relative technological resource applicability increases dramatically in its impact, generating the fourth-largest effect of all independent variables on estimated probability of mode choice. While this is a far cry from the dominant effect of technological applicability on the direction of diversification, it underscores the role played by technological relatedness in firms' decisions about mode of entry.

Conclusion

Prior theoretical work concerning the mode of diversification has generated a widely held belief that the relatedness of a diversification move influences entry mode selection. However, no prior empirical test of which I am aware has found any significant relationship between measures of relatedness and mode choice. Through the use of relatedness measures that are consistent with my contentions in Chapters 2 and 3 – specifically, that exploration of the resource-based framework necessarily must rely on direct measures of resource characteristics such as range of applicability – this study has uncovered a modest but significant relationship between technological resource applicability and mode choice for technology-intensive firms. The results extend my understanding in two ways. First, they suggest that a firm's technological resource base, as manifested in its corporate patent portfolio, significantly influences its diversification mode choice. Second, they are further evidence of the value of

Table 6.6 Changes in estimated probabilities of entry (effect of changing independent variable from mean value to 1 standard deviation above the mean) (3)

Variable (units)	Full sample					Technology-intensive subsample				
	Mean	1 std. dev. above mean	P(entry | var. at 1 std. dev. above mean)[a]	Change from P(entry | var. at mean)[a]	Rank in importance	Mean	1 std. dev. above mean	P(entry | var. at 1 std. dev. above mean)[a]	Change from P(entry | var. at mean)[a]	Rank in importance
IGrowth (%)	11.104	16.449	0.585	+0.045	5	11.417	16.764	0.638	+0.061	3
IConc (%)	33.817	53.459	0.593	+0.053	4	35.041	55.334	0.606	+0.029	7
IR&DS (%)	2.242	4.519	0.457	−0.083	2	2.298	4.528	0.475	−0.101	2
IAdvS (%)	1.315	3.466	0.506	−0.034	8	1.178	3.168	0.572	−0.004	11
FSales ($B)	5.458	19.247	0.567	+0.027	10	7.460	23.736	0.612	+0.035	6
Growth (%)	5.000	15.901	0.472	−0.068	3	5.569	16.409	0.493	−0.083	5
FR&DS (%)	1.743	3.372	0.672	+0.132	1	1.835	3.350	0.721	+0.145	1
FAdvs (%)	1.181	3.437	0.508	−0.032	9	0.927	2.809	0.575	−0.002	10
DiffR&D (%)	1.615	3.392	0.576	+0.036	7	1.641	3.427	0.605	+0.029	8
DiffAdv (%)	1.503	3.813	0.501	−0.039	6	1.293	3.425	0.534	−0.042	9
WgtAbsTech (patents)	6.790	36.491	0.555	+0.015	12	9.706	45.241	0.568	−0.009	12
WgtRelTech (patents)	0.072	0.217	0.561	+0.021	11	0.071	0.204	0.629	+0.099	4

Note
a Assuming all other variables are held constant at their mean values.

Table 6.7 Changes in estimated probabilities of entry (effect of changing independent variable from median value to third quartile) (4)

	Full sample					Technology-intensive subsample				
Variable (units)	Median	Third quartile	P(entry | var. at third quartile)[a]	Change from P(entry | var. at median)[a]	Rank in importance	Median	Third quartile	P(entry | var. at third quartile)[a]	Change from P(entry | var. at median)[a]	Rank in importance
IGrowth (%)	10.665	13.639	0.558	+0.025	5	11.090	14.270	0.594	+0.037	4
IConc (%)	31.000	43.000	0.566	+0.033	4	32.000	44.500	0.575	+0.018	7
IR&DS (%)	1.390	3.010	0.474	−0.059	2	1.550	3.050	0.489	−0.068	2
IAdvS (%)	0.630	1.600	0.526	−0.007	10	0.640	1.000	0.556	−0.001	10
FSales ($B)	1.833	4.899	0.539	+0.006	11	3.292	5.914	0.563	+0.006	9
Growth (%)	2.954	10.571	0.486	−0.048	3	2.954	9.784	0.504	−0.053	3
FR&DS (%)	1.199	2.376	0.631	+0.098	1	1.435	2.397	0.654	+0.097	1
FAdvs (%)	0.175	1.259	0.518	−0.015	7	0.000	1.098	0.556	−0.001	10
DiffR&D (%)	0.996	2.173	0.557	+0.024	6	1.034	2.214	0.576	+0.019	6
DiffAdv (%)	0.684	1.490	0.520	−0.013	8	0.640	1.067	0.548	−0.008	8
WgtAbsTech (patents)	0.476	3.150	0.535	+0.001	12	1.312	5.419	0.556	−0.001	10
WgtRelTech (patents)	0.016	0.069	0.541	+0.007	9	0.020	0.069	0.576	+0.020	5

Note
a Assuming all other variables are held constant at their median values.

identifying the underlying characteristics of specific pools of resources to understand the role these resources have in contouring firm behavior.

In addition, this chapter includes the first test of which I am aware that explores, albeit indirectly, a fundamental yet implicit assumption of prior empirical research on the mode of diversification: the underlying nature of the diversification decision process.

7   Conclusion

This study has examined the influence of technological resources on corporate diversification in the US manufacturing sector. The concluding chapter summarizes the major results and discusses their implications for competitive strategy, technology strategy, the resource-based view of the firm, and future research.

Summary of major results

The resource-based view of the firm has provided a potentially powerful lens through which to view corporate diversification. A growing body of research has suggested that a firm's diversification behavior is largely driven by its resource pool. This study has extended the extant research in three ways. First, it has operationalized technological resources at a more microanalytic level and from a different perspective than previous research. In so doing, it has presented a novel method to identify businesses in which a given patent can provide competitive value. Second, it has explicitly incorporated transaction cost concepts about contractual alternatives to diversification. Third, it has extended the range of research questions addressed by the resource-based view, in particular by deriving hypotheses concerning the mode of diversification.

Technological resources can be effectively operationalized through the use of highly detailed, publicly available data. Chapter 4 described the relative advantages of patent data as compared to traditional R&D statistics or innovation counts, arguing that patents, while by no means perfect, offer an attractive measure of technological resources. Chapter 4 then developed, both conceptually and empirically, a novel technique to link patents to businesses in which they are likely to provide competitive utility. This technique was tested against existing methodologies for such linkage, and was found to be superior in terms of accuracy and level of detail.

This study hypothesized that a firm's diversification pattern can be explained by examination of a few attributes that characterize its resource base: (1) the specific (narrow) range of businesses in which the resources offer competitive utility, (2) the feasibility of their exploitation through non-diversification (i.e., contractual) means, and (3) the sustainability of these resources. The first two of these were tested in Chapter 5 with data on 2514 diversification entries and non-entries made by US manufacturing firms between 1981 and 1985. Armed with the patent–business linkage methodology developed in Chapter 4, I determined the extent to which each firm's patent portfolio was applicable to the target industries. Through the use of the Yale study on innovation (Levin *et al.* 1987), I determined the feasibility of exploiting technological resources through contractual mechanisms (i.e., licensing) in these target industries. The results supported both hypotheses: a firm is significantly more likely to diversify into businesses in which its existing technological resource base provides competitive advantage, and significantly less likely to do so if licensing is feasible.

A firm can diversify through one of several modes. While there has been a general consensus among management scholars that the choice between acquisition and internal expansion is somehow mediated by the relatedness of the diversification entry, the few prior empirical studies of this topic have not found a significant relationship. Chapter 3 proposed that specific attributes of the firm's resources – notably, the extent to which they are applicable to a new business and the rate at which they are created – affect the mode by which a firm diversifies. Chapter 6 provided an empirical analysis of this proposition, relying again on the operationalization of resource attributes derived earlier in the thesis. This analysis, based on 1023 diversifying entries between 1981 and 1985, indicated that among technology-intensive firms, a diversifying firm is moderately more likely to choose internal expansion over acquisition the more applicable its pool of technological resources is to the target industry.

In summary, this study represents one of the most extensive attempts thus far to theoretically and empirically operationalize resource attributes. This study extends the resource-based view's reach by addressing questions about the mode of diversification. This study is also one of the first explicitly to incorporate transaction cost economics into the resource-based framework.

Implications for future research

Additional attributes of resources deserve further analysis. The theoretical analysis in Chapter 3 argued that the sustainability of a resource influences the likelihood that a firm will attempt to exploit that resource. The empirical analysis in this thesis, however, did not test this hypothesis.

Attributes of other resources affecting the firm's diversification decision also need further empirical analysis. Chapter 3 suggested that a number of non-technological resources, such as marketing resources, brand names, and production knowledge, might be important. Chapter 5 provided some tentative evidence about the effect of such factors, in that similarity in advertising intensities between firm and target industry (a proxy for marketing resources and brand names) has a positive and significant effect on diversification. However, rigorous operationalization of these resources was beyond the scope of this study. Further efforts to operationalize attributes of these resources is warranted.

This study used fairly crude measures to identify industries in which licensing of technological resources was likely (or not likely) to be feasible. However, there is growing evidence that a wide range of rich institutional arrangements may be devised to govern the exploitation of resources (Pisano 1990; Powell 1990; Hergert and Moriss 1988). Future research would benefit from a focus on these arrangements and their attendant institutional details.

Future research on the resource-based implications of diversification should also attempt to capture the performance consequences of diversification moves.[1]

Finally, future research on the resource-based view of the firm should attempt to differentiate empirically between the conventional resource-based (resources as stocks) frameworks and the dynamic capabilities (resources as flows) approach. Much heat has been generated by the theoretical debate between resource-based and capabilities scholars, but little light will be provided without empirical analysis of longitudinal data on the accumulation, exploitation, and dissipation of resources. The Trinet data and patent data described in this study, which respectively cover spans of ten years and fifteen years, offer substantial promise for such analysis.

Implications for managers

The theory and evidence provided in this study suggest that a firm's technological resource base provides a logic for the direction and mode of corporate diversification. Managers can and should examine the attributes of their existing resource bases to determine business opportunities where they may enjoy competitive advantage. In addition, managers can examine the attributes of other firms' resource bases to identify potential competitors. Finally, contractual arrangements to exploit resources – even resources commonly assumed to suffer from contractual hazards – may offer viable alternatives to diversification.

In more pragmatic terms, the patent–business mapping methodology developed and tested in this thesis may prove useful to practitioners. A large number of firms are presently undertaking efforts to identify and exploit their core technological competences (Stewart 1994). Practitioners may find that mapping their patent portfolios into businesses of likely utility will provide them with insights into potential avenues to leverage their technological resources. In addition, mapping competitors' patent portfolios could provide managers with early warning of potential competitive threats. In the long run, the ultimate test of academic research in management must be its utility to those who practice the managerial arts. I hope that the results of this investigation will prove to be of at least some value in this regard.

Appendix 1 Comparison of Scherer and patent concordance assignment of patents (top three patents from concordance)

Matches at four-digit SIC level

Patent number	Technology	Assignee	Scherer assignment	Patent concordance assignment (top 3)	
				Use	Mfre
3960872	Antihistamine and appetite stimulant compounds	Merck	2831, 2833, 2834	2834 2833 2831	2869 2899 2865
3961369	Rotating head apparatus for magnetic tape recording	IBM	3651	3651 3573 3662	3651 3662 3679
3962430	Sterilization of medicinal agents employing sodium chloride	Merck	2831, 2833, 2834	2834 2844 2833	2834 2844 2833
3963001	Combustion system for internal combustion engines	Black & Decker	3546, 3519	3711 3569 3519	3714 3599 3519
3963644	Conversion catalysts for hydrocracking	Union Oil	2911	2869 2899 2911	2869 2899 2865
3964094	Improvements to rotating head magnetic tape reader	IBM	3573, 3571, 3577	3651 3573 3662	3651 3662 3679
3964844	Vane pump	Parker Hannafin	3561, 359	3711 3561 3585	3561 3563 3564
3965209	Selective production of para-xylene	Mobil Oil	2865, 2869	2869 2834 3079	2869 2865 2899
3966429	Improved manganese-containing fuels	Sohio	2911	2951 2952 2911	2911 2951 2952
3966965	Oxamic acid derivatives for the prevention of hypersensitivity reactions	American Home Products	2831, 2833, 2834	2834 2844 2833	2834 2844 2833
3970452	Ion modulator device and methods for copy production	Addressograph	3861	3573 3861 3579	3573 3861 3579

Patent number	Technology	Assignee	Scherer assignment	Patent concordance assignment (top 3)	
				Use	Mfre
3970876	Voltage and temperature compensation circuitry	Burroughs	3573, 3574	3662 3661 3573	3662 3661 3679
3971575	Releasable locking device for brake system	Combined Engineering	3443	3079 3711 3443	3494 3317 3079
3972046	Antenna arrangement for a submerged submarine	ITT	3662, 3661, 3669	3662 3661 3622	3662 3661 3679
3972706	Herbicidal method	Eli Lilly	2879	2491 2879 2869	2879 2869 2865
3973133	Ozone generator	General Tire	2865, 2869, 376	2819 2899 2874	2819 2899 2869
3973873	Negative torque sensor for a gas turbine engine	Atlantic Richfield	3724	3721 3724 3728	3721 3724 3728
3974305	Treatment of strontium chloroapatite to improve fluorescent lamps	Westinghouse	3641	3651 3661 3641	3662 3641 3679
3975073	Fluorescent lampholder	Westinghouse	3645, 3646, 3641	3662 3622 3661	3662 3641 3679
3975528	Novel insecticide derivatives	American Cyanamid	2879	2491 2879 2869	2879 2869 2865
3977963	Method of negating effects of metals poisoning on cracking catalysts	Gulf Oil	2911	2911 2951 2952	3531 3533 3519
3978446	Electric cable hydrophone array for undersea exploration	GTE	3662	3494 3662 3661	3662 3494 3622
3979557	Speech processor system for pitch period extraction	ITT	3661	3662 3573 3661	3662 3573 3661
3981497	Document feed apparatus	IBM	3573, 3571, 3577	3573 3861 2611	3573 3861 3519
3981928	Perfluorotertiaryalkyl ethers	3M	2865, 2869	2869 2834 3079	2869 2865 2899
3982958	Non-aqueous battery system	Union Carbide	3691, 3692	3694 3691 3648	3694 3691 3648
3983346	Gas circuit breaker	ITE	3613, 3625	3622 3662 3679	3613 3662 3679

Patent number	Technology	Assignee	Scherer assignment	Patent concordance assignment (top 3)	
				Use	Mfre
3983870	Slip-resistant body limb support	3M	3841, 3842	2221	3842
				3842	3861
				2253	3494
3984421	Novel central nervous system depressants	Squibb	2831, 2833, 2834	2834	2869
				2833	2865
				2831	2899
3984967	Mechanical safety interlock for preventing mower operation during reverse travel	Allis Chalmers	3524	3523	3523
				3524	3524
				3519	3519
3985968	Multiplex data communications	IBM	3573, 3662	3662	3662
				3661	3679
				3679	3661
3987107	Conversion of methanol to formaldehyde	E.I. DuPont	2865, 2869	2869	2869
				2834	2865
				3079	2899
3988649	Signal amplitude monitor	GE	3613, 3625	3622	3613
				3662	3662
				3679	3679
3989366	Photoelectrophoretic imaging apparatus for color copies	Xerox	3861	3573	3573
				3861	3861
				3579	3579
3989771	Rubbermodified styrene polymers	Standard Oil	2821, 2822	3079	3079
				2821	2821
				2851	2869
3991968	Quick release seat retainer clamping device	Chrysler	3711, 3713	3711	3494
				3599	3599
				3519	3714
3992432	Phase transfer catalysis	Continental Oil	2865, 2869	2869	2869
				2834	2865
				3079	2899
3994917	Oxazolinium salt process to make ketones	Eli Lilly	2831, 2833, 2834	2834	2869
				2833	2865
				2831	2899
3996032	Insulated heater tray for making glass fibers and method for using same	PPG Inds	3229	3231	3231
				3229	3221
				3221	3229
3997007	Hydraulic control system for positioning implement	Caterpillar	3531	3531	3531
				3523	3533
				3533	3599
3997519	Method of producing quarternary pyridinium compounds	GAF	2865, 2869	2899	2869
				2869	2865
				2865	2899
4000703	Trough hatch locking device	Pullman	3743	3519	3519
				3462	3462
				3743	3743
4001237	Amides for anti-hypertension drug	Bristol-Myers	2831, 2833, 2834	2834	2869
				2833	2865
				2831	2899

Patent number	Technology	Assignee	Scherer assignment	Patent concordance assignment (top 3)	
				Use	Mfre
4001693	Apparatus for establishing communication between two radio transmitter/receivers	GE	3662	3662 3661 3573	3662 3661 3622
4003909	Antibacterial/antifungal compounds	Squibb	2831, 2833, 2834	2834 2833 2831	2869 2865 2899
4004416	Infra-red suppressor to protect military aircraft from infra-red-seeking missiles	UTC	3721, 3728	3721 3724 3728	3721 3724 3728
4005027	Scouring compositions	Procter & Gamble	2841, 2842, 2843	2841 2842 3291	2841 2842 3291
4007205	Compounds to fight asthma and hay fever	Warner Lambert	2831, 2833, 2834	2834 2833 2831	2869 2899 2865
4008376	Loudspeaking teleconferencing unit	AT&T	3661	3661 3662 3679	3661 3662 3679
4009031	Diffusion transfer image-receiving element to reduce haze in photos	Polaroid	3861	3573 3861 3579	2869 3861 2865
4009448	Phase lock loop for a voltage controlled oscillator (e.g., radar system)	Westinghouse	3662	3662 3651 3661	3662 3679 3661
4011711	Device to form bales of crop material	Sperry Rand	3523	3523 3524 3519	3523 3524 3519
4012699	Device to amplify optical signals	AT&T	3661	3662 3661 3494	3662 3679 3494
4013442	Process for encapsulation with a metal carbonate coating	Exxon	2873, 2874, 2875	2875 2819 2874	2875 2879 3429
4015077	Facsimile transmitter having improved response	Exxon	3662, 3661, 3669	3651 3662 3661	3651 3662 3661

Matches at three-digit SIC level

				Patent concordance assignment (top 3)	
Patent number	*Technology*	*Assignee*	*Scherer assignment*	*Use*	*Mfre*
3968092	Chloroprene polymer vulcanization accelerators	E.I. DuPont	282	3079 2821 2869	3079 2869 2821
3982371	Panel holding structure	Scovill	243	2431 3442 3711	3442 3231 3079
3985586	Phosphoric acid soldering flux	Allegheny Ludlum	331, 3469, 3449	3622 3714 3317	3622 3621 3511
3987600	Fire-resistant doors	U.S. Gypsum	3442	3272 3448 2452	3448 3272 3079
4006140	Vulcanizable rubber compositions involving morpholinothio oxamides	Goodrich	2822	2834 2833 2821	2865 2869 2899
4012328	Acid soluble packer and workover fluid	Dresser	289 × 2892, 3533	2869 3079 3641	2869 2865 2899

Matches at two-digit SIC level

				Patent concordance assignment (top 3)	
Patent number	*Technology*	*Assignee*	*Scherer assignment*	*Use*	*Mfre*
3962092	Screen changer	Dow	2821, 307	2869 2819 2899	3519 3569 3559
3965847	Service minder odometer	GM	3711, 3713	3662 3494 3721	3662 3494 3679
3967532	Forward-reverse valve for elevating scraper drive	Caterpillar	3531	3711 3599 3519	3494 3599 3714
3968624	Connector fixture	GTE	344 × 3445–7	3711 3429 3494	3495 3429 3079
3969651	Plasma display panel system	IBM	3573, 3671	3646 3585 3645	3622 3662 3621

Patent number	Technology	Assignee	Scherer assignment	Patent concordance assignment (top 3)	
				Use	Mfre
3976278	Valve assembly for measuring spinal fluid pressure	Colgate	3841, 3842	3494 3519 3711	3494 3825 3079
3980321	Hitch pin assembly for a tractor-scraper vehicle and the like	Caterpillar	3531	3711 3715 3792	3523 3714 3715
3980852	Adjustable high-density cam-switch assembly	Litton	3693–99, 384	3622 3662 3679	3613 3662 3679
3986614	Tray and elevator mechanism for handling signatures	Harris Intertype	3555, 3423	3531 3533 3519	3531 3533 3519
3990906	Cleaning tire molds by ultrasonic wave energy	Goodyear	301	3585 2869 3079	3585 3519 3411
3991313	Method and apparatus for acoustically monitoring neutron flux radiation	Westinghouse	382, 3443	3662 3494 3599	3494 3861 3662
3992953	Accelerometer using radioactive pickoff	Singer	3811	3711 3494 3825	3494 3662 3825
3995426	Mechanical linkage for hydrostatic control system	Caterpillar	3531	3711 3599 3519	3494 3599 3714
3999690	Metering apparatus for a seed planter	White Motor	3523	3079 3519 2869	3079 3494 3519
4002375	Railway vehicle brake control valve	American Standard	3743	3711 3519 3714	3714 3519 3079
4003427	Heat pipe fabrication	Grumman	376	3443 3585 3711	3443 3585 3494
4005524	Method of making an antenna connector	Chromalloy	3675, 3679, 3264	3622 3662 3661	3641 3357 3662
4006666	Cushioning device for a hydraulic jack	Caterpillar	3537	3711 3599 3519	3494 3599 3714
4007814	Carbon brake disk with cast keyslot reinforcement members	Goodyear	3721, 3728	3711 3599 3519	3714 3599 3079
4010097	Pneumatic classifier for refuse material with double vortex airflow (to sort trash by weight)	Allis Chalmers	358 × 3585	3519 3559 3569	3519 3559 3569

Patent number	Technology	Assignee	Scherer assignment	Patent concordance assignment (top 3)	
				Use	Mfre
4010640	Apparatus for measuring the stiffness characteristic of structural adhesives	American Cyanamid	289 × 2892	3494 3825 3823	3494 2834 3825
4011213	Chemical compounds useful as fungicides and mite ovicides	E.I. DuPont	2879	2869 2834 3079	2869 2865 2899

No match at two-digit SIC level

Patent number	Technology	Assignee	Scherer assignment	Patent concordance assignment (top 3)	
				Use	Mfre
3969223	Olefin separation process	Universal Oil Products	7000–8900	2911 2951 2952	3531 3533 3519
3976718	Powder coating compositions comprising a blend of coreactive polymers	Ford	3711, 3713	3079 2821 2851	3079 2821 2869
3977217	Friction twist knitting machine element	Ingersoll Rand	396, 3999	2257 2258 2328	2257 2258 3519
3979179	Process and composition for reducing evaporation of volatile liquids	Anheuser Busch	2082, 2046	2869 2899 2911	2869 2899 2865
3988216	Method of producing metal strip while preventing formation of zinc deposit on cathode means	National Steel	331	3471 3479 3661	3471 3479 2869
3990191	Method for removal of paper from dye springs	Burlington Inds	221–223, 225	3714 3519 3851	3519 3569 3559
3993661	Photographic reagent compounds	Polaroid	3861	2834 2833 2831	2869 2865 2899
3994244	Fluidized waste incinerator and method	Shell Oil	2813	3585 2911 3731	3585 3634 3564
3996466	Transfer corona device with adjustable shield bias for xerography	Xerox	3861	3711 3079 3714	3613 3714 3622
3998031	Apparatus and method for the preparation of enclosed sanitary products	W.R. Grace	2647, 2821	3519 2086 3559	3519 3569 3559

Patent number	Technology	Assignee	Scherer assignment	Patent concordance assignment (top 3)	
				Use	Mfre
3998667	Barium aluminoborosilicate glass-ceramics for semiconductor doping	Owens–Illinois	3293–99, 3229	3662 3679 3661	3662 3679 3661
3999062	Spectrophotometer for dual mode fluorescence analysis	IBM	3573	3662 3679 3494	3494 3851 3825
4000206	Process for the production of benzene, cyclohexane and motor fuel	Phillips Oil	2911	2869 2834 3079	2869 2865 2899
4002829	Autosynchronous optical scanning and recording laser system with fiber optic light	W.R. Grace	3555, 3079, 3423	3651 3662 3661	3651 3662 3661
4013872	Temperature control device	Mobil Oil	2911	3648 3585 3645	3622 3662 3661
4014638	Photoflash lamp with electrostatic protection and method of making photoflash units	GTE	3641	2099 2086 2011	2099 2869 2041

Note
X = excluding

Appendix 2 Sample firms

Cusip	Company	Cusip	Company
1030	AEL Industries	75887	Becton Dickinson & Co
1688	AMF Inc	76635	Beech Aircraft Corp
1723	AM International Inc	77455	Belden Corp
2824	Abbott Laboratories	81437	Bemis Co
4626	Acme-Cleveland Corp	87509	Bethlehem Steel Corp
7603	Aegis Corp	87779	Betz Laboratories Inc
7842	Aeronca Inc	90527	Binks Mfg Co
9158	Air Products & Chemical	90763	Bird Corp
10202	Akzona	91797	Black & Decker Corp
12347	Albany Intl Corp	97023	Boeing Co
13068	Alberto-Culver Co	97383	Boise Cascade Corp
22249	Aluminum Co of America	99599	Borden Inc
23519	Amerace Corp	109043	Briggs & Stratton
24703	American Brands Inc-Del	115223	Brown & Sharpe Mfg Co
25321	American Cyanamid Co	117043	Brunswick Corp
26609	American Home Products	117421	Brush Wellman Inc
26681	American Hospital Suppl	120547	Bundy Corp
27339	American Maize-Prods	120655	Bunker Ramo Corp
27627	American Motors Corp	121690	Burlington Ind Eqty
29465	American Seating Co	123655	Butler Mfg Co
30087	American Sterilizer Co	124800	CBI Industries Inc
30710	Ameron Inc-Del	124884	CCI Corp
31105	Ametek Inc	126149	CPC International Inc
31897	Amp Inc	126501	CTS Corp
32087	Ampex Corp	127055	Cabot Corp
33047	Anchor Hocking Corp	134429	Campbell Soup Co
33609	Anderson Clayton & Co	134449	Campbell Taggart Inc
42627	Aro Corp	142339	Carlisle Cos Inc
43339	Arvin Industries Inc	143483	Carnation Co
44540	Ashland Oil Inc	146285	Carter-Wallace Inc
47483	Athlone Inds	149123	Caterpillar Inc
48825	Atlantic Richfield Co	150843	Celanese Corp
54303	Avon Products	157177	Cessna Aircraft Co
58498	Ball Corp	158663	Champion Spark Plug
67131	Barber-Greene Co	165339	Chesebrough-Pond's Inc
68887	Barry Wright Corp	167898	Chicago Pneumatic Tool
71707	Bausch & Lomb Inc	171106	Chromalloy American Corp

Cusip	Company	Cusip	Company
171196	Chrysler Corp	277461	Eastman Kodak Co
172172	Cincinnati Milacron Inc	278058	Eaton Corp
181396	Clark Equipment Co	278749	Echlin Inc
186757	Clevepak Corp	281347	Edo Corp
189000	Clopay Corp	285551	Electronic Associates Inc
189054	Clorox Co-Del	291011	Emerson Electric Co
189468	Clow Corp	291210	Emhart Corp
191216	Coca-Cola Co	296470	Esmark Inc
194162	Colgate-Palmolive Co	296659	Esquire Inc
194828	Collins & Aikman Corp	296695	Essex Chemical Corp
200273	Combustion Engineering	297425	Esterline Technologies
207192	Congoleum Corp	297659	Ethyl Corp
208251	Conoco Inc	300587	Ex-Cell-O Corp
209759	Consolidated Papers Inc	302290	Exxon Corp
211452	Continental Group	302491	FMC Corp
212363	Control Data Corp	307387	Farah Inc
212813	Conwed Corp	313135	Fedders Corp
216669	Cooper Industries Inc	313549	Federal-Mogul Corp
216705	Cooper Laboratories	313855	Federal Signal Corp
216831	Cooper Tire & Rubber	315405	Ferro Corp
217016	Coors (Adolph)	316549	Fieldcrest Cannon
217210	Copeland Corp	318315	Firestone Tire & Rubber
219093	Cornelius Co	337693	Fischer & Porter Co
219350	Corning Inc	339711	Flintkote Co
224399	Crane Co	345370	Ford Motor Co
227111	Crompton & Knowles Corp	351604	Foxboro Co
227813	Crouse-Hinds Co	353514	Franklin Electric Co
229890	Culbro Corp	359694	Fuller (H.B.) Co
231021	Cummins Engine	361614	GF Corp
231561	Curtiss-Wright Corp	361765	GK Technologies Inc
235773	Dan River Inc	367410	Gates Learjet Corp
235811	Dana Corp	369550	General Dynamics Corp
236289	Danly Machine Corp	369604	General Electric Co
237424	Dart Industries	370118	General Instrument Corp
238107	Dataproducts Corp	370334	General Mills Inc
244199	Deere & Co	370442	General Motors CL E
248631	Dennison Mfg Co	370622	General Refractories Co
249028	Dentsply International	370838	General Signal Corp
250595	De Soto Inc	373712	Gerber Products Co
250685	Detrex Corp	375046	Giddings & Lewis Inc
252165	Dexter Corp	375766	Gillette Co
252579	Diamond Crystal Salt Co	377316	Glatfelter (P.H.) Co
253651	Diebold Inc	382388	Goodrich (B.F.) Co
253849	Digital Equipment	382550	Goodyear Tire & Rubber
260543	Dow Chemical	383492	Gould Inc
260561	Dow Jones & Co Inc	383883	Grace (W.R.) & Co
261597	Dresser Industries Inc	399820	Grow Group Inc
263534	Du Pont (E.I.) De Nemou	400181	Grumman Corp
266849	Duriron Co Inc	402784	Gulton Industries Inc
268039	Dynamics Corp of Amer	404245	HMW Industries Inc
268163	Dyneer Corp	413345	Harnischfeger Industries

Cusip	Company	Cusip	Company
413875	Harris Corp	543213	Longview Fibre Co
415864	Harsco Corp	543859	Loral Corp
418056	Hasbro Inc	547779	Lowenstein (M.) Corp
420758	Hayes-Albion Corp	549271	Lubrizol Corp
421596	Hazeltine Corp	549662	Ludlow Corp
423074	Heinz (H.J.) Co	552618	M/A-Com Inc
423236	Helene Curtis Inds	559108	Magic Chef Inc
427056	Hercules Inc	561229	Mallinckrodt Inc
427866	Hershey Foods Corp	564402	Mansfield Tire & Rubber
428236	Hewlett-Packard Co	565821	Marathon Mfg Co
429812	High Voltage Engineering	570385	Mark Controls Corp-Old
433728	Hobart Corp	573275	Martin Marietta Corp
438506	Honeywell Inc	574055	Maryland Cup Corp
439272	Hoover Co	574599	Masco Corp
440452	Hormel (Geo. A.) & Co	575379	Masonite Corp
444356	Huffy Corp	577081	Mattel Inc
448510	Huyck Corp	577896	Mayer (Oscar) & Co
449168	Hyster Co	579780	McCormick & Co
449290	ICN Pharmaceuticals Inc	580169	McDonnell Douglas Corp
451542	Ideal Basic Industries	580628	McGraw-Edison Co
451650	Ideal Toy Corp	582562	McNeil Corp
452308	Illinois Tool Works	582699	McQuay Inc
456866	Ingersoll-Rand Co	584404	Media General
459200	Intl Business Machines	586005	Memorex Corp
459550	Intl General Industries	589331	Merck & Co
460043	Intl Multifoods Corp	589433	Meredith Corp
460146	Intl Paper Co	597715	Midland-Ross Corp
460254	Intl Rectifier Corp	601753	Milton Bradley Co
460578	Interpace Corp	602720	Mine Safety Appliances
465632	Itek Corp	604059	Minnesota Mining & Mfg
478160	Johnson & Johnson	608030	Mohasco Corp
478366	Johnson Controls Inc	608302	Mohawk Rubber Co
481070	Joslyn Corp	611662	Monsanto Co
486746	Kearney & Trecker Corp	615394	Moog Inc
487836	Kellogg Co	619600	Mosinee Paper Corp
489170	Kennametal Inc	620076	Motorola Inc
492386	Kerr-McGee Corp	626320	Munsingwear Inc
492710	Keuffel & Esser Co	627151	Murray Ohio Mfg Co
493422	Keystone Cons Industries	628862	NCR Corp
494368	Kimberly-Clark Corp	629156	NL Industries
497656	Kirsch Co	629853	NALCO Chemical Co
500170	Koehring Co	630854	NARCO Scientific Inc
500440	Kollmorgen Corp	637742	National-Standard Co
501206	Kuhlman Corp	656389	Norris Industries Inc
501858	LFE Corp	666807	Northrop Corp
502210	LTV Corp	668605	Norton Co
513696	Lamson & Sessions Co	671400	Oak Industries Inc
524462	Leesona Corp	680665	Olin Corp
532253	Lightolier Inc	682063	Omark Industries Inc
532457	Lilly (Eli) & Co	690020	Outboard Marine Corp
538021	Litton Industries Inc	690734	Owens Corning Fiberglass

Cusip	Company	Cusip	Company
690768	Owens-Illinois Inc	826622	Signal Cos
693506	PPG Industries Inc	826690	Signode Corp
693715	Pabst Brewing Co	831865	Smith (A.O.) Corp
698635	Pantasote Inc	832377	Smithkline Beckman Corp
701094	Parker-Hannifin Corp	833034	Snap-on Tools Corp
704225	Paxall Inc	835852	Sorg Paper Co
705041	Peavey Co	847235	Sparton Corp
709317	Pennwalt Corp	848355	Sperry Corp
714041	Perkin-Elmer Corp	851783	Springs Industries
716723	Petrolite Corp	852206	Square D Co
717081	Pfizer Inc	852245	Squibb Corp
724479	Pitney Bowes Inc	852308	Sta-Rite Industries
730026	Plymouth Rubber	852864	Stanadyne Inc
731095	Polaroid Corp	853037	Standard Alliance Industries
736202	Portec Inc	853734	Standard Oil Co
737628	Potlatch Corp	853887	Standard Register Co
742718	Procter & Gamble Co	854412	Stange Co
746252	Purex Industries Inc	854616	Stanley Works
747402	Quaker Oats Co	855668	Starrett (L.S.) Co
749285	RCA Corp	857721	Stauffer Chemical Co
751277	Ralston Purina Co	858586	Stepan Co
752159	Ranco Inc	859264	Sterling Drug Inc
754603	Raychem Corp	860486	Stewart-Warner Corp
755111	Raytheon Co	861589	Stone Container Corp
758556	Reeves Brothers Inc	866762	Sun Co Inc
759200	Reichhold Chemicals Inc	867323	Sundstrand Corp
759457	Reliance Electric Co	867833	Sunshine Mining Co
759574	Remington Arms Co	871140	Sybron Corp
761406	Revere Copper & Brass Inc	872649	TRW Inc
761763	Reynolds Metals Co	878895	Tecumseh Products Co
763121	Richardson Co	879131	Tektronix Inc
766481	Riegel Textile Corp	879335	Teledyne Inc
766626	Riley Co	879573	Telex Corp
770196	Robbins & Myers Inc	881694	Texaco Inc
770519	Robertshaw Controls	882508	Texas Instruments Inc
770706	Robins (A.H.) Co	883203	Textron Inc
774347	Rockwell Intl Corp	884102	Thiokol Corp
775371	Rohm & Haas Co	884425	Thomas Industries Inc
775422	Rohr Inc	887389	Timken Co
781088	Rubbermaid Inc	889073	Tokheim Corp
784015	SCM Corp	890278	Tonka Corp
784626	SPS Technologies Inc	891067	Torin Corp
793453	St Regis Corp	891092	Toro Co
799850	Sanders Associates Inc	892892	Trane Co
806605	Schering-Plough	902120	Tyco Laboratories Inc
806823	Schlitz (Jos.) Brewing	902184	Tyler Corp/Del
809877	Scott Paper Co	904790	UNIMAX Corp
810640	Scovill Inc	905530	Union Camp Corp
812302	Searle (G.D.) & Co	905581	Union Carbide Corp
819139	Shakespeare Co	909160	Uniroyal Inc
824348	Sherwin-Williams Co	910365	United Foods

Cusip	Company	Cusip	Company
910671	United Industrial Corp	953348	West Co Inc
913017	United Technologies Corp	955465	West Point-Pepperell
915302	Upjohn Co	958264	Western Gear Corp
918314	VSI Corp	960402	Westinghouse Electric Corp
920355	Valspar Corp	961548	Westvaco Corp
922204	Varian Associates Inc	962166	Weyerhaeuser Co
922272	Varo Inc	962898	Wheelabrator-Frye
922612	Vendo Co	963320	Whirlpool Corp
927770	Virginia Chemicals Inc	963626	White Consolidated Inds
933169	Walter (Jim) Corp	974637	Winnebago Industries
934408	Warner & Swasey Co	977385	Witco Corp
934459	Warner Elec Brake & CLU	982526	Wrigley (Wm.) Jr Co
934488	Warner-Lambert Co	983085	Wyman-Gordon Co
942486	Watkins-Johnson	984121	Xerox Corp
947015	Wean Inc-PA	989349	Zenith Electronics Corp
949765	Wells-Gardner Electronics		

Notes

1 Introduction

1 While there are many different types of diversification – into new geographic markets; into new lines of business; into new customer segments – unless otherwise specified I use the term to refer to diversification into new lines of business.

2 As Rumelt (1974) chronicled, the percent of Fortune 500 companies in his sample that were single business corporations fell from 35 percent in 1949 to 6 percent in 1969. Teece et al. (1994: 7) use data concerning all establishments in the US with twenty or more employees, which suggests a population of more than 18,000 multi-product firms in the United States in 1987.

3 For example, Gort (1962), Didrichsen (1972), Chandler (1977), MacDonald (1985), and Montgomery and Wernerfelt (1988).

4 See for example Rumelt (1974), Montgomery (1981), Singh and Montgomery (1987).

5 Notably Caves et al. (1980), Palepu (1985), Jacquemin and Berry (1979), Gollop and Monahan (1991).

6 Prior studies that have relied on one or more years of Trinet data include Wernerfelt and Montgomery (1988), Chatterjee and Wernerfelt (1991), Teece et al. (1994), and Singh and Subbanarasimha (1993).

7 Trinet claimed to collect information on virtually every establishment with 20 or more employees. Comparisons of this database to data compiled by the US Census of manufactures suggests that Trinet accurately identified more than 95 percent of the establishments which it should have identified (Voigt 1993). See Voigt (1993) for an extensive description of the Trinet database's strengths and weaknesses.

8 Streitwieser (1991: 507) found that, according to Census of Manufactures data, less than 3 percent of all establishments in the US encompass more than three four-digit SIC businesses.

9 This study used an extract of the PATDAT database, which included every patent issued by the Canadian Patent Office between 1978 and 1987. I am extremely grateful to Professor Sam Kortum for making this extract available to me.

2 Review of prior theoretical and empirical research on diversification

1 Other economic explanations of diversification have emphasized risk management (Coffee 1988), agency problems (Jensen 1986), predation (Levy 1989) and mutual forbearance (Edwards 1955; Scott 1982; Bernheim and Whinston 1990). In addition, organization theory has offered explanations that stress the importance of diversification to managing dependence on resources (Pfeffer and Salancik 1978) and the influence of structural holes on multiproduct operations (Burt 1992). See Baum and Korn (1994) for an ecologically motivated view of diversification and multimarket contact.

2 It is interesting to note that, while Penrose's work is almost always cited as an antecedent of modern evolutionary economics (see for example Nelson and Winter 1982; Teece 1982, 1988), Penrose herself was highly skeptical of the direct application of biological theory to economics (Penrose 1952, 1953).

3 The Penrosian notion of disequilibrium should be distinguished from the modern definition, which suggests *unanticipated* change. In the Penrosian framework, disequilibrium refers to the fact that the firm at time t + 1 will not have identical productive capacity, and hence will not make the same production decisions, as it does at time t. Experience curve models (e.g., Fudenberg and Tirole 1983) may be interpreted as examples of this sort of disequilibrium pressure.

4 At the same time, there are limits to the amount a firm can expand at any given point in time. These constraints are primarily a function of the amount of time the firm's managers can allocate to managing growth.

5 At the same time, one could argue that the transaction cost framework explicitly recognizes (as does agency theory) that self-interested managers may be reluctant to give up control over corporate assets even if such divestment is the most "efficient" course in the absence of adequate disciplinary devices.

6 It is also difficult to see how financial resources on their own can attract rent. Chatterjee and Wernerfelt's assertion that financial resources facilitate unrelated diversification seems more properly evidence of managerialism along the lines of Jensen's theory of free cash flow (Jensen 1986) or the earlier managerial discretion literature (Berle and Means 1932; Williamson 1964).

7 For example, Barney's treatment of key resource factor markets (1986) can be interpreted as focusing on resource stocks rather than resource flows (Dierickx and Cool 1989, but see Barney 1989 for a response). Wernerfelt (1984) and Chatterjee and Wernerfelt (1991) generally treat resources as pre-existing stocks upon which to formulate strategy, although Wernerfelt (1984) does briefly propose a strategy of business entry predicated on the gradual accumulation of resources.

8 The terminology by which these rival camps identify themselves stems from Penrose (1959), who defined resources as "a bundle of potential services [that] can, for the most part, be defined independently of their use" and capabilities as "services of resources [which] cannot be so defined, the very word 'service' implying a function, an activity" (Penrose 1959: 25; see also Mahoney and Pandian 1992: 366).

9 It is hoped that the longitudinal databases compiled for this study will in the future prove useful to the empirical comparison of the resource-based vs. capabilities views.

10 As measured by the fraction of all firm personnel who were involved in R&D activities.

11 Although some studies have found that higher R&D intensity is not always positively correlated with increased diversification (for a summary of these see Scherer 1980), as Pavitt *et al.* (1989) point out, much of the discrepancy is likely due to the measures and levels of aggregation employed.

12 Teece's analysis relies heavily on subjective rather than objective measures of similarity, reflecting the great difficulty of developing objective measures at any level of detail greater than, say, R&D intensity.

13 Wrigley's categorization consisted of single product, dominant, related, and unrelated.

14 Resource-based theorists have argued that related diversifying acquisitions should yield more favorable capital market responses than unrelated acquisitions, all else equal.

15 Synergy could occur in sales (due to common distribution), operations (due to ability to spread overhead and exploit transferable learning curves), investment (through common inventories) or management (due to transferable experience) (1965: 80). Ansoff also noted that diversification into an unrelated industry could actually create "negative synergy" to the extent that the new business is beset by problems alien to the experience of existing management.

16 Scholars such as Pitts (1976, 1977) and Lamont and Anderson (1985) have also examined issues associated with diversification mode. However, these studies ignore the determinants of modal choice, focusing instead on whether simultaneous pursuit of diversification by acquisition and by internal growth is feasible. Similarly, Pennings *et al.* (1994) explore the effect of diversification mode on subsequent divestment, but do not examine the determinants of mode choice. Several international business scholars have examined modal choice in foreign market entry – i.e., under what conditions does a firm build a foreign subsidiary through acquisition of a foreign company rather than through greenfield development (Hennart and Park 1993; Kogut and Singh 1988; Caves and Mehra 1986). These studies view foreign expansion as different in kind from domestic expansion, and largely deal with non-diversifying expansion (i.e. expanding existing business operations to a new country).

17 According to Yip, certain entry barriers differentially raise the cost of internal expansion more than that of acquisition. For example, since entry by internal expansion entails adding capacity in the target industry while entry by acquisition does not, Yip hypothesized that firms entering stagnant or low-growth industries will favor acquisition over internal expansion, *ceteris paribus*.

18 For that matter, only two out of five entry barrier variables had significant effects in the expected direction: market growth and incumbent parent size. Two other entry barrier variables, concentration and advertising intensity, were predicted to be insignificant and were indeed insignificant. While this conforms to Yip's model, it does not support the contention that entry barriers have an effect on diversification mode.

19 In spite of this focus on resources, Chatterjee measured relatedness as proximity in the SIC system, which (as described earlier in this chapter) is somewhat at odds with resource-based assumptions.

20 Chatterjee did, however, find evidence for capital market imperfections that drive the firm's diversification mode decision. It should also be noted that Chatterjee found that increased market growth had a significant and negative effect on diversification by internal growth – the opposite effect noted by Yip.

21 The results of Amit *et al.* arguably provide modest support for (1) the transaction cost notion (as developed by Teece 1982) that the rate at which excess resources are created affects the modal decision, and (2) the evolutionary economics argument that firms which have diversified by acquisition in the past are likely to diversify by acquisition in the future. However, these empirical tests include virtually no control variables and are based on rather heroic assumptions (which the authors acknowledge).

22 "A firm becomes superior in a particular technological domain because it has certain organizational capabilities: it allocates resources to more promising projects, it harnesses experience from prior projects, it hires and upgrades human resources, it integrates new findings from external sources, and it manages a set of problem-solving activities associated with that technology" (Dosi and Teece 1993: 6–7).

23 "Firms cannot change their position in technology space overnight, but … over some horizon they do move in response to perceived profit opportunities" (Jaffe 1986: 997).

24 Such a linkage is the subject of Chapter 4.

25 Singh and Subbanarasimha (1993) comment on the desirability of such a detailed characterization in their conclusion.

26 Most of the above-cited studies of diversification–performance linkage use the direction of diversification as the primary characteristic by which performance should vary. Two exceptions are Montgomery and Wernerfelt (1988) and Wernerfelt and Montgomery (1988), which also consider the overall scope of diversification.

3 The effect of resource attributes on the direction, mode, and performance of corporate diversification

1　Or, put another way, these resources will only generate rents in a limited range of applications.

2　As Pisano (1988: 64) notes, "Licensing of future improvements [after an initial contract] is subject to opportunism. The licensee's technology specific capital is a source of quasi-rents for the licensor. Knowing that the licensee has sunk specialized capital into the technology, the licensor can extract higher royalties for future 'improvement licences.'"

3　Similarly, resources related to distribution may fall along a continuum from easy-to-difficult to contract out. Anderson and Schmittlein (1984) and Anderson (1988) find that transaction cost considerations largely explain the make-or-buy decision in sales forces.

　　Another interesting question relates to whether different classes of resources occupy different areas on the continuum from low to high contractual hazards. One might conjecture that resources related to distribution, such as access to particular channels, are relatively easy to contract out as compared to technological resources, and that production-related resources fall somewhere in between.

4　This is a standard assumption of transaction cost economics and the resource-based view of the firm.

5　Dierickx and Cool (1989) discuss five attributes of resources that determine their sustainability: time compression diseconomies (i.e., "crash" R&D programs are less efficient than long-term research investments; therefore a technological lead can be difficult to erode); asset mass efficiencies (i.e., in a market where word-of-mouth is important, cumulative sales may be an important determinant to current sales); interconnectedness of asset stocks (i.e., product improvements may be sparked by customer feedback, so the firm with the most customers has an advantage in gaining new ideas); asset erosion (i.e., the rate of decay of R&D or brand awareness affects the credibility of entry deterrence by a resource-endowed firm); and causal ambiguity (i.e., if rivals cannot identify which factors facilitate a firm's asset accumulation process, then they cannot imitate the firm's asset position).

6　This closely parallels the prevailing wisdom since Ansoff (1965).

7　A semi-strong efficient capital market implies that all resources are fairly valued on the basis of publicly available information.

8　Conversely, diversification into a business far removed from management's range of experience is likely to incur above-average startup costs (what Ansoff 1965 calls "negative synergy").

9　It may be the case that not all related diversification is designed to exploit economies of scope. Nayyar (1993) argues that some related diversification is designed to exploit information asymmetry in experience goods. For example, a reputable accounting firm will diversify into consulting because potential clients, who cannot easily determine in advance the ability of the consultants, will hire them on the basis of the firm's accounting competence. The implications for integration and centralization remain largely the same, however, in that shared reputational capital can be diluted by divisional actions that do not adequately take into account interdivisional spillover effects.

10　Indeed, Hill *et al.* (1992) argue that an unrelated diversifier, in order to function properly as an internal capital market (Williamson 1975), must impose interdivisional competition rather than cooperation. Such competition relies on divisional autonomy and discourages interdivisional integration.

11　In his discussion of the advantages of the M-form structure, Williamson (1975: 153) points out that two subcategories of M-form firms are usefully distinguished, one of which is "a highly integrated M-form enterprise, possibly with differentiated but otherwise common final products," and the other being "the M-form enterprise with diversified final products or services." Williamson concludes that "a more extensive internal control apparatus to manage spillover effects is needed in the former." The framework presented above, while emphasizing common resources rather than common final products, is not inconsistent with Williamson's treatment of the subject.

12　In a study of international expansion, Kogut and Singh (1988) find that the internal growth is increasingly favored over acquisition as nation-level cultural distance increases.

13　The significance of the results in Hill *et al.* (1992) depends somewhat on the measure of diversification employed.

　　Several other studies have contrasted the organizational structure of firms that have grown through internal expansion to those that have grown via acquisition. Pitts (1976, 1980) and Berg (1973) have found that firms that rely on internal expansion tend to (1) maintain larger corporate staffs, especially in R&D, (2) design promotion ladders that expose their manager to more divisions, and (3) provide managerial incentives based more heavily on subjective criteria rather than the objective financial parameters most closely associated with the M-form conglomerate. Large corporate R&D staffs are presumably required to manage supra-divisional technical resources. Promotion ladders that expose managers to several divisions and incentive systems that rely on subjective criteria are likely to facilitate interdivisional cooperation and coordination rather than competition. However, these studies did not test for performance differences between those firms that conform to these regularities and those that do not.

14　This can also be presented mathematically as follows: Let startup cost S be parameterized as a function of relatedness r, where r is defined as relatedness between firm i's existing resources and the resource requirements of entered industry j. Then $\partial S_{\text{acquisition}}(r)/\partial r > 0 > \partial S_{\text{internal expansion}}(r)/\partial r$, because firm i's cost of obtaining needed resources is reduced as its existing resources are more applicable to industry j (see p. 21), while firm i's cost associated with acquiring redundant assets is expected to increase as its existing resources are more applicable to industry j (see p. 21). At the same time, $S_{\text{acquisition}}(0) = S_{\text{internal expansion}}(0) = 0$. Let integration costs I also be parameterized as a function of relatedness r. Then $\partial I_{\text{acquisition}}(r)/\partial r > \partial I_{\text{internal expansion}}(r)/\partial r > 0$, because the need for integration increases as the relatedness between existing and new operations increases and the cost (difficulty) of integration is higher for acquisition than for internal expansion (see p. 22). At the same time, $I_{\text{acquisition}}(0) = I_{\text{internal expansion}}(0) = 0$. Thus, diversifying entries characterized by high levels of relatedness will be more cheaply effected through internal expansion. Entries characterized by low levels of relatedness will be effected through acquisition or internal expansion at relatively similar cost, on average.

4　Patent data and construction of a US patent class–SIC concordance

1　The stochastic models add a random component to innovation by drawing success (or failure) of innovation at a given point in time from a poisson distribution. Nevertheless, the underlying distribution is parameterized as a function of R&D expenditure.

2　This assumption would violate the resource-based framework in two ways. First, since the idea that a "menu" exists of new technologies from which all firms may draw is assumed to be incorrect (Nelson and Winter 1982), for any specific technology some firms will be more able than others to convert R&D into innovations. Second, some firms may simply have a generic "capability" to innovate (Teece *et al.* 1994; Dosi and Teece 1993), which suggests that different firms have different R&D-to-technical-output cost curves.

3 To reiterate a point made in the previous chapter, many resource-based studies of diversification have cited the fact that firms with high R&D intensities tend to enter industries with high R&D intensities as evidence of resource-driven diversification, arguing that high firm R&D expenditures indicate the existence or development of technical resources which the firm can exploit in other industries that value such technical resources. However, this characterization of technical resources does not allow us to predict whether a pharmaceutical firm is more likely to diversify into biotechnology or into telecommunications, as both of these industries are characterized by high R&D expenditure.

4 Data on scientific personnel at the industry level can be compiled more readily. The Occupational Employment Survey, conducted by the Bureau of Labor Statistics, collects information on the distribution of employees in 480 distinct occupations at the three-digit SIC level (Farjoun 1994).

5 Some trade journals regularly include announcements of new products (for example, *Semiconductor Age* and *Solid State Technology* in the semiconductor and semiconductor manufacturing equipment industries), but these comprise only a small and somewhat biased subsection of all innovations. While such sources are useful for studies of new product introduction (e.g., Henderson 1988), they are of less value when confronted with more general research questions concerning underlying technical resources.

6 For a complete description of patent issuance criteria, see the US Patent Act, as amended, part II: Patentability of Inventions.

7 Roughly 70 percent of all patent applications which will eventually be granted are granted within three years of the application date, and about 97 percent by four years after application (Griliches *et al.* 1987).

8 No public information is available for patent applications that are rejected by the USPTO.

9 Patents are typically granted to individual inventors. Inventors can assign these patent rights to other individuals or to organizations. It is standard practice for a company's researcher to assign patents to her employer upon granting. Of all patents granted to US applicants (about 60 percent of all patents granted in the early 1980s, and about 50 percent today), nearly three-fourths are assigned to a corporation.

10 The limited evidence available concerning the timing of invention and patent application suggests that firms typically file patent applications between six and nine months after invention (Schmookler 1966; Scherer 1982a).

11 Patents cannot encompass all inventive output because some technical knowledge is uncodifiable (e.g., tacit knowledge) or otherwise unpatentable (e.g., algorithms). In addition, a firm that is concerned about revealing technical knowledge in its patent applications may choose not to patent all of its patentable technology.

12 Yet another concern is that there may be differences at the firm, industry, or temporal level in the proportion of patents that are commercially exploited (Sanders 1964; Schmookler 1966).

13 Although, as stated before, one would expect that even the most insignificant patent has (for the applicant) an expected return which exceeds the cost of obtaining a patent.

14 Patent renewal fees were introduced in the US in 1980, due at $3\frac{1}{2}$, $7\frac{1}{2}$, and $11\frac{1}{2}$ years after granting.

15 Carpenter *et al.* used the 1969 and 1970 IR 100 Award recipient list – those products identified by a panel of experts assembled by the journal *Industrial Research and Development* as the most technologically significant of the year – as the basis for their technically important patent sample.

16 Patents can be assigned to industries in at least two ways: to the industry in which the patented innovation is manufactured (aptly called "industry of manufacture") and to the industry in which the patented innovation will be used ("industry of

use"). In addition, one can identify the industry in which the patented innovation was developed ("industry of origin"), which is often but not always the industry of manufacture or industry of use (Schmookler 1966; Griliches 1990).

17 Schmookler illustrated this with the following examples: "Within a main class which deals with dispensing liquids is a subclass containing, among other things, a patent for a holy water dispenser. Another patent in the same subclass is for a water pistol. Again, in a subclass within a main class covering the dispensing of solids, one patent was on a manure spreader, another, on a toothpaste tube" (1966: 20, footnote 4). A more recent study noted that the same patent subclass contains innovations pertaining to both windmills and egg beaters (OTAF 1985).

18 Scherer assigned industries based on the Federal Trade Commission's Line of Business classification system, which corresponds fairly closely to the SIC system at the $3\frac{1}{2}$ digit level. (See US Federal Trade Commission 1977, Appendix D, for a concordance between lines of business and standard industry classifications.)

19 "The productivity impact of new products is observed 'downstream' at the buying and using industry stage, both because the prices measured for inputs used by the buying industries do not reflect their superiority value and because (thanks to competition) the prices actually paid do not reflect that superiority value" (Scherer 1984b: 423).

20 Scherer actually drew every 150th patent (arranged in numerical order) from his sample rather than drawing a truly randomly generated sample. He argued that the apparently stochastic nature of patent issuance order ensured that this yielded a sufficiently random sample (Scherer 1982b).

21 For example, Economic Council of Canada (1971) and Firestone (1971).

22 "As originally conceived, PATDAT was developed to fulfill three functions:
   1 to provide data necessary to the formulation of concrete proposals for revision of Canada's Patent Act;
   2 to provide data for use by researchers in assessing the economic implications of patents, in particular, the social costs and benefits of patent protection; and
   3 to provide data for use by industry and government in assessing technological trends and the downstream success or failure of R&D programs."
   (Ellis 1981; see Ellis 1981 for an extensive description of the PATDAT database)

23 Other information not normally available in patent data that is available in PATDAT includes whether the patent covers a product or a process, and whether or not the patent covers a cost-saving innovation.

24 Patent officers can assign a patent to as many as three SICs of use, in descending order of likelihood. However, the vast majority of Canadian patents are assigned to one SIC. There is also a catch-all class called "General Utility" to which patent officers can assign the few patents which defy SIC classification, such as ball-bearings (Ellis 1981).

25 Patent officers can assign a patent to as many as three SICs of manufacture, in descending order of likelihood. As with SICs of use, however, the vast majority of Canadian patents are assigned to one SIC. The literature on PATDAT betrays some confusion over the meaning of SIC of manufacture. Many describe it as conforming to Schmookler's definition – that is, it is the industry in which the patented product is likely to be manufactured (Ellis 1981; Kortum and Putnam 1989a). Others, however, treat it as conforming to Griliches' definition of industry of origin – that is, the industry in which the innovation is made (Englander *et al.* 1988). As Griliches (1990) has pointed out, the industry of origin and the industry of manufacture need not be the same. Thus, while PATDAT's industry of manufacture "may be a convenient, though imperfect, proxy for the industry of 'origin'" (Kortum and Putnam 1989a: 2, footnote 3), care must be taken in using this data. Studies of technological flows across industries that rely on PATDAT for industry of origin data will be incorrect to the extent that SIC of manufacture differs from SIC of origin.

26 Evenson and Putnam (1988) outline the construction of an IPC–SIC concordance for use within Canada. Kortum and Putnam (1989a, 1989b) suggest that this may be extended outside of Canada. Englander *et al.* (1988) use this concordance concept to discuss technology flows in OECD countries.

27 Kortum and Putnam claim to allow inference of patenting in countries other than Canada, but their model and empirical work retains Canadian industry classification. This precludes effective economic analysis by industry for those countries whose SIC systems differ from that of Canada.

28 In the PATDAT data, of course, there are two SICs to which a patent may be applicable – that of use and that of manufacture. This analysis is limited to one for convenience.

29 Although such differences would cast doubt on the depiction of technology pools presented above. See Kortum and Putnam (1989b) for more on this case.

30 I am grateful to F.M. Scherer for providing me with his individual line of business assignments for these patents.

31 Note that this would not be an identity matrix unless every US four-digit SIC industry also mapped into exactly one Canadian four-digit SIC industry.

32 Officials in the USPTO discourage reliance on the IPC assigned to individual patents, asserting that US patent examiners are not particularly expert at understanding the subtleties of the IPC system and that such individual assignments can introduce subjective error. As was pointed out during the discussion of PATDAT above, however, subjective error may be a small price to pay for individual patent assignment.

33 It may also be worth noting that the three patents assigned to automobile manufacturers fared poorly in terms of matches (one matched at the two-digit level; two did not match at all). In contrast, patents assigned to firms primarily involved with telecommunications and computers tended to yield matches at the three- and four-digit level.

5 An empirical analysis of the effect of technological resources on the direction of corporate diversification

1 Montgomery and Hariharan, in turn, borrow from Lemelin (1982).

2 I do not include a direct measure of industry profitability as did Montgomery and Hariharan, because reliable data on industry profitability is not available for the time period covered by my data. However, this is not as severe a lack as it first appears. Most studies of diversification have not included an industry profit measure. More important, the two that have (Montgomery and Hariharan 1991; Orr 1974) both found that industry profitability has an insignificant effect on diversification entry when factors that are hypothesized to affect industry profitability (such as industry concentration, growth, advertising intensity, and R&D intensity) are included as variables. I include these factors as variables.

3 I used the 1972 Standard Industrial Classification System, which was in effect during the years of this study.

4 During this time, the firm went under the names EIS and Trinet. In 1991 Trinet was acquired by ABI, which stopped collecting and publishing the Trinet database in a format similar to that of the Trinet data.

5 See Voigt (1993) for an extensive description of the Trinet database's strengths and weaknesses.

6 Potential entries = 412 firms × 429 industries − 6027 firm-industry participation pairs existing in 1981 = 170,721.

7 As with most statistical research in management, I will actually be testing a null hypothesis which states that there is *not* a relationship between technological resources and the direction of diversification. A positive significant coefficient for $AbsTech_{ij}$ will thus enable me to reject the null hypothesis in favor of Hypothesis 1.

8 Two-year, four-year, and five-year compound annual growth rates were also used. Results did not change significantly with these alternative specifications.

9 Eight-firm concentration ratios were also used. Results did not change significantly with this alternative specification.

10 In addition, my firm-level R&D intensity variable is based upon the four years 1978 through 1981, which should further reduce any potential discrepancy incurred by using 1976 industry-level R&D data.

11 Two-year, four-year, and five-year compound annual growth rates were also used. Results did not change significantly with these alternative specifications.

12 A potential criticism of this measure is that, in much resource-based work, it is the firm's growth *relative* to the growth of the industries in which it currently participates that influences its diversification decision (see Gort 1962; Penrose 1959). Future work in this area could incorporate such a measure. In the meantime, however, it is worth noting that even Penrose, who elsewhere suggests the importance of the firm-growth/industry-growth connection, argues that unless excess resources were generated in a perfectly "balanced" fashion – that is, so that they may be recombined for use in current operations with no resources left over – diversification would remain a desirable option regardless of current industry growth (Penrose 1959). Working under the assumption that higher-growth is more likely to yield a resource imbalance than lower growth, many resource-based scholars have used firm growth as the relevant measure (see for example Montgomery and Hariharan 1991).

13 I also constructed a R&D intensity variable using the firm's total assets as the denominator. Results were not significantly different.

14 Two-year averages and 1981-only data were also used. Results were not significantly different.

15 I also constructed an advertising intensity variable using the firm's total assets as the denominator. Results were not significantly different.

16 Two-year averages and 1981-only data were also used. Results were not significantly different.

17 Respondents to the Yale survey were generally vice-presidents or directors of R&D for SBUs of Fortune 500 firms.

18 The Yale survey asked respondents to rate the effectiveness of royalties as an appropriation mechanism separately for process and for product innovations. I have averaged both ratings in this measure. This is also true for the other appropriability measures described below.

19 As stated above, such a coefficient is more accurately interpreted as a rejection of the null hypothesis that contracting hazards have no effect on diversification.

20 Note that the rationale for the learning curve's positive effect on diversification differs from that of secrecy. Where the importance of secrecy is assumed to proxy for the difficulty of retaining proprietary knowledge – the paradox of information (Arrow 1971) – the importance of learning curve effects is assumed to proxy for the difficulty of transferring tacit knowledge (Teece 1982).

21 The logit model assumes that the probability distribution corresponds to a logistic curve. The probit model assumes that the underlying probability distribution corresponds to a normal distribution. These logistic and normal distributions are similar except for their tails; consequently, unless a large proportion of observations are clustered in the tails, estimation results should not be greatly affected by choice of functional form.

22 The constant term can be modified by subtracting from it the following value:

ln [proportion of observations in state 1 that are included in the sample/proportion of observations in state 2 that are included in the sample].

In my estimation sample, I include all entries and 0.9 percent (1491 out of 170,721) of the non-entries. The adjustment for my constant term is therefore ln[0.009] = −4.710. Conceptually, this adjusts the constant, and thus the maximum likelihood function overall, for the fact that while I estimate the entry process for a sample in which more than 40 percent of the observations are entries, in reality the probability of any entry taking place is extremely small.

23　While a 10 percent improvement may not sound substantial, it is instructive to note that the addition of all other variables to a baseline model containing only the constant term improves the explanatory power by only 25 percent. (A baseline model consisting of only a constant term predicts all observations to be non-entries, which yields 1023 errors. Model 1, which includes all conventional variables plus the constant yields 762 errors, thus cutting the error rate by 25 percent.)

24　Since concentration has a negative effect on diversification, its value is set at one standard deviation above the mean.

25　Note that the estimated probabilities calculated in this section are for the sample and not for the population. The constant term has not been adjusted to account for the effects of state-based sampling. For the population overall, the probability of entry when all variables are set to their means is less than 1 percent, rising to slightly more than 9 percent when WgtAbsTech is set at one standard deviation above its mean.

26　Since IConc has a negative effect on the probability of entry, I used its value at one standard deviation *below* the mean.

27　Decreasing IR&DS and IAdvS by one standard deviation would create values below zero. Since these measures cannot be less than zero, I set them equal to zero.

28　The primary difference is that FR&DS falls to insignificance in the constrained sample results, due to the higher standard error associated with the decreased number of observations.

29　It is worth noting that the Yale measures have frequently exhibited weak explanatory power in empirical research applications of this sort because of their low dispersion across industries (see for example Cockburn and Griliches 1987, 1988). The modest results found in this study are more impressive when viewed against this context.

30　Other sources included research equipment suppliers, universities, and the government.

31　Alternative cutoffs, such as above the third quartile, were also tried. Results tended to be similar, but significance was reduced due to the reduced number of observations.

32　Given the parameters used by Jaffe to select his sample, these populations overlap substantially. I also used 20 patents and 100 patents as patent portfolio cutoff points, with no change in the results.

6 An empirical analysis of the effect of technological resources on the mode of corporate diversification

1　In other words, to avoid the "early mistakes" (Ansoff 1965) that often plague managers in unfamiliar territory.

2　Chatterjee (1990), in the only other empirical study to examine modal choice for individual diversification moves, used the Caves concentric index (described in Chapter 2) to measure relatedness of each entry.

3　I also include R&D intensity data, which Yip discusses but does not include in his empirical test.

4　Some of the establishment codes in 1979 are different from their 1981–1989 counterparts. Voigt (1993) has devoted considerable effort to reconciling these discrepancies, and can be contacted for more information on this subject. The present study focuses only on post-1981 data and therefore is not affected by the 1979 data problem.

5　There were 17 instances where a firm's entry into an industry – which can be a multi-establishment entry – included both internal expansion and acquisition. For these cases I assigned an entry to whichever mode accounted for more establishments (or, in the case of a tie, more employees). For all but three of these 17 cases, the number of plants involved in one mode exceeded the number of plants involved in the other mode by a ratio of 2:1 or more.

6 The discerning reader will notice that industry sales is not included as a variable in this specification although it was included in Chapter 5. While I had reason to believe that industry size would affect probability of entry into an industry, there is no a priori rationale to predict that the size of an industry should affect diversification mode. Inclusion of the industry sales variable in this model yielded an insignificant coefficient, and estimations including $ISales_j$ are not shown in the exhibits.

7 Eight-firm concentration ratios were also used. Results did not change significantly with this alternative specification.

8 This may be more likely with related acquisitions.

9 Yip (1982) found that entrant parent size did not have a significant effect on entry mode. He attributed this result to the conflicting effects of firm size described above. He does not present descriptive statistics in his paper, but I conjecture that his data, which consisted of 59 entries by firms in the PIMS database, might not have included a wide range of entrant firm sizes. A general uniformity in firm size would reduce the likelihood of finding a significant relationship. In contrast, my entrants range from less than $20 million to over $100 billion in sales.

10 This has become known as the "Penrose effect." For empirical evidence of the Penrose effect, see for example Slater (1980) and Shen (1970).

11 Yip's sample consisted of only 59 entries, 37 of which were internal expansions. Yip identified entry by surveying competitors of the new entrant rather than the new entrant itself. It is possible that data provided by these observers is distorted or incomplete. Further, Yip excluded acquisitions in which the acquiree's goal was to "merely hold [the acquired business] as a portfolio investment" rather than intending "to use the acquired business as a base for expansion" (apparently based on the inference of its competitors). It is not clear how many acquisition entries Yip discarded due to this exclusionary rule, but the effect would be to increase the proportion of internal expansions among all entries. Chatterjee (1990) identified diversified entries through the Fortune Plant Directory of 1968. He then determined the mode of entry through a search of secondary sources such as Annual Reports and *Wall Street Journal* announcements. If no reference to an acquisition in the entered business appeared in the secondary sources, then Chatterjee defined the entry as internal growth. It is possible that Chatterjee's use of internal growth as his default category explains at least in part the higher incidence of internal growth in his sample as compared to mine.

12 Such an examination is beyond the scope of this chapter and would make an interesting paper in its own right.

13 Note that this test does not confirm that the traditional model is the most accurate alternative. It merely finds that one potential alternative model is potentially valid or is not potentially valid.

14 See Maddala (1983) and Hausman and McFadden (1984) for more details.

15 Note that the vector and matrix for the unconstrained estimation exclude the elements that are eliminated (assumed to equal zero) in the constrained estimation.

16 Likelihood ratio test statistic = 2* [log-likelihood(unconstrained) − log-likelihood

$$\text{(constrained)}]$$
$$= 2*\,[-651.198 - -653.955]$$
$$= 4.515$$

7 Conclusion

1 The Trinet data could support studies of de-diversification of between eight and ten years.

Bibliography

Acs, Z.J., D.B. Audretsch, and M. Feldman (1994), "R&D spillovers and recipient firm size," *Review of Economics and Statistics* 100(1), February.

Alchian, A. (1950), "Uncertainty, evolution and economic theory," *Journal of Political Economy* 58: 211–221.

Amit, R., J. Livnat, and P. Zarowin (1989), "The mode of corporate diversification: Internal ventures versus acquisitions," *Managerial and Decision Economics* 10: 89–100.

Amit, R. and P.J.H. Schoemaker (1993), "Strategic assets and organizational rent," *Strategic Management Journal* 14: 33–46.

Anderson, E. (1988), "Transaction costs as determinants of opportunism in integrated and independent sales forces," *Journal of Economic Behavior and Organization* 9: 247–264.

Anderson, E. and D.C. Schmittlein (1984), "Integration of the sales force: An empirical examination," *Rand Journal of Economics* 15(3): 385–395.

Annual Survey of Manufactures (various years), Washington, DC: US Department of Commerce, Bureau of the Census.

Ansoff, H.I. (1965), *Corporate Strategy*, New York: McGraw-Hill.

Ansoff, H.I., R.G. Brandenburger, F.E. Portner, and R. Radasovich (1971), *Acquisition Behavior of U.S. Manufacturing Firms, 1946–1965*, Nashville: Vanderbilt University Press.

Argyres, N.S. (1995), "Technology, strategy, governance structure and interdivisional coordination," *Journal of Economic Behavior and Organization* 28: 337–358.

Arrow, K.J. (1971), *Essays on the Theory of Risk-Bearing*, Chicago: Markham.

Barney, J.B. (1986), "Strategic factor markets: expectations, luck, and business strategy," *Management Science* 32: 1230–1241.

Barney, J.B. (1989), "Asset stocks and sustained competitive advantage – a comment," *Management Science* 35: 1511–1513.

Barney, J.B. (1991), "Firm resources and sustained competitive advantage," *Journal of Management* 17(1): 99–120.

Baum, J.A.C. and H.J. Korn (1994), "Competitive dynamics of interfirm rivalry: Linking structural conditions of competition to patterns of market entry and exit," Unpublished manuscript, University of Toronto.

Baumol, W.J., J. Panzar, and R. Willig (1982), *Contestable Markets*, New York: Harcourt Brace Jovanovich.

Baysinger, B. and R.E. Hoskisson (1989), "Diversification strategy and R&D intensity in multiproduct firms," *Academy of Management Journal* 32(2): 310–322.

Berg, N.A. (1973), "Corporate role in diversified companies," in B. Taylor and K. MacMillan (eds), *Business Policy: Teaching and Research*, New York: Wiley.

Berle, A.A. and E.C. Means (1932), *The Modern Corporation and Private Property*, New York: Macmillan.

Bernheim, B.D. and M.D. Whinston (1990), "Multimarket contact and collusive behavior," *Rand Journal of Economics* 21(1), Spring: 1–26.

Bernstein, J.I. and M.J. Nadiri (1988), "Interindustry R&D spillovers, rates of return, and production in high-tech industries," *American Economic Review* 78(2): 429–434.

Berry, R. (1974), "Corporate diversification and market structure," *Bell Journal of Economics* 5: 196–204.

Bettis, R.A. (1981), "Performance differences in related and unrelated diversified firms," *Strategic Management Journal* 2: 379–393.

Biggadike, E.R. (1979), *Corporate Diversification: Entry, Strategy, and Performance*, Boston: Division of Research, Graduate School of Business Administration, Harvard University.

Bound, J., C. Cummins, Z. Griliches, B. Hall, and A. Jaffe, "Who does R&D and who patents?" in Z. Griliches (ed.), *R&D, Patents and Productivity*, Chicago: University of Chicago Press.

Burt, R. (1992), *Structural Holes: The Social Structure of Competition*, Cambridge: Harvard University Press.

Carpenter, M., F. Narin, and P. Woolf (1981), "Citation rates to technically important patents," *World Patent Information* 3(4): 160–163.

Caves, R.E. (1987), "Exports of manufactures from developing countries – performance and prospects for market access – Cline, W.R.," *Annals of Regional Science* 21: 155–157.

Caves, R.E. and S. Mehra (1986), "Entry of foreign multinationals into U.S. manufacturing industries," in M.E. Porter (ed.), *Competition in Global Industries*, Boston: Harvard Business School Press.

Caves, R.E., M.E. Porter, and A.M. Spence (1980), *Competition in the Open Economy*, Cambridge: Harvard University Press.

Census of Manufactures (1982), Washington, DC: US Department of the Census.

Census of Manufactures (1987), Washington, DC: US Department of the Census.

Chandler, A.D. (1977), *The Visible Hand: The Managerial Revolution in American Business*, Cambridge: Belknap/Harvard University Press.

Chandler, A.D. (1990), *Scale and Scope: The Dynamics of Industrial Capitalism*, Cambridge: Belknap/Harvard University Press.

Chandler, A.D. (1992), "Organizational capabilities and the economic history of the industrial enterprise," *Journal of Economic Perspectives* 6(3): 79–100.

Chatterjee, S. (1990), "Excess resources, utilization costs, and mode of entry," *Academy of Management Journal* 33(4): 780–800.

Chatterjee, S. and B. Wernerfelt (1991), "The link between resources and type of diversification: Theory and evidence," *Strategic Management Journal* 12: 33–48.

Christensen, H.K. and C.A. Montgomery (1981), "Corporate economic performance: diversification strategy vs. market structure," *Strategic Management Journal* 2: 327–343.

Cockburn, I. and Z. Griliches (1987), "Industry effects and appropriability measures in the stock market's valuation of R&D and patents," *NBER Working Paper No. 2465*, December.

Cockburn, I. and Z. Griliches (1988), "Industry effects and appropriability measures in the stock market's valuation of R&D and patents," *American Economic Review* 78(2): 419–423 [abridged version of 1987 NBER Working Paper].

Coff, R.W. and D.E. Hatfield (1995), "A resource-based view of value creation in acquisitions: An expertise-based measure of relatedness," Paper presented at the Academy of Management meeting, Vancouver, August.

Coffee, J.C. (1988), "Shareholders vs. managers: The strain in the corporate web," in J.C. Coffee, L. Lowenstein, and S. Rose-Ackerman (eds), *Knights, Traders and Targets: The Impact of the Hostile Takeover*, New York: Oxford University Press.

Cohen, W.M. and D.A. Levinthal (1990), "Absorptive capacity: A new perspective on learning and innovation," *Administrative Science Quarterly* 35(1): 128–152.

Comanor, W. and F.M. Scherer (1969), "Patent statistics as a measure of technical change," *Journal of Political Economy* 77(3): 329–398.

Conner, K.R. (1991), "A historical comparison of resource-based theory and 5 schools of thought within industrial organization economics: Do we have a new theory of the firm?" *Journal of Management* 17(1): 121–154.

Davis, R. and I.M. Duhaime (1992), "Diversification, vertical integration, and industry analysis: new perspectives and measurement," *Strategic Management Journal* 13: 511–524.

Didrichsen, J. (1972), "The development of diversified and conglomerate firms in the United States, 1920–1970," *Business History Review* 46(2): 202–219.

Dierickx, I. and K. Cool (1989), "Asset stock accumulation and sustainability of competitive advantage," *Management Science* 35(12): 1504–1514.

Dosi, G. and D.J. Teece (1993), "Organizational competencies and the boundaries of the firm," *CCC Working Paper No. 93–11*, University of California at Berkeley, Haas School of Business.

Dunne, T., M.J. Roberts, and L. Samuelson (1988), "Patterns of firm entry and exit in U.S. manufacturing industries," *Rand Journal of Economics* 19(4): 495–515.

Economic Council of Canada (1971), *Report on Intellectual and Industrial Property*, Ottawa: Economic Council of Canada.

Edwards, C.D. (1955), "Conglomerate bigness as a source of power," in NBER Conference Report, *Business Concentration and Price Policy*, Princeton: Princeton University Press.

Edwards, K.L. and T.J. Gordon (1984), "Characterization of Innovations Introduced in the U.S. Market in 1982," The Futures Group.

Ellis, E.D. (1981), "Canadian Patent Data Base: The philosophy, construction, and uses of the Canadian patent data base PATDAT," *World Patent Information* 3(1): 13–18.

Englander, A.S., R.E. Evenson, and M. Hanazaki (1988), "R&D, innovation and the total factor productivity slowdown," *OECD Economic Studies* 11: 8–42.

Evenson, R.E. and J. Putnam (1988), "The Yale–Canada concordance," Unpublished manuscript, Yale University Economic Growth Center.

Farjoun, M. (1994), "Beyond industry boundaries: human expertise, diversification and resource-related industry groups," *Organization Science* 5(2), May: 185–199.

Firestone, O. (1971), *Economic Implications of Patents*, Ottawa: University of Ottawa Press.

Frame, J.D. and F. Narin (1990), "The United States, Japan, and the changing technological balance," *Research Policy* 19(5): 447–455.

Freeman, C. (1982), *The Economics of Industrial Innovation*, London: Pinter.

Fudenberg, D. and J. Tirole (1983), "Learning by doing and market performance," *Bell Journal of Economics* 14: 522–530.

Gilbert, R. and D. Newbery (1982), "Preemptive patenting and the persistence of monopoly," *American Economic Review* 72: 514–526.

Gollop, F.M. and J.L. Monahan (1991), "A generalized index of diversification: trends in U.S. manufacturing," *Review of Economics and Statistics* 73: 318–330.

Gort, M. (1962), *Diversification and Integration in American Industry*, Princeton: Princeton University Press.

Gort, M. and S. Klepper (1982), "Time paths in the diffusion of product innovations," *Economic Journal* 92, September: 630–653.

Griliches, Z. (1990), "Patent statistics as economic indicators: A survey," *Journal of Economic Literature* 28, December: 1661–1707.

Griliches, Z., A. Pakes, and B.H. Hall (1987), "The value of patents as indicators of economic activity," in P. Dasgupta and P. Stoneman (eds), *Economic Policy and Technological Performance*, Cambridge: Cambridge University Press.

Hagedoorn, J. and G. Duysters (1993), "The Cooperative Agreements and Technology Indicators (CATI) Information System," Unpublished manuscript, Maastricht, The Netherlands, MERIT.

Hausman, J., B.H. Hall, and Z. Griliches (1984), "Econometric models for count data with an application to the patents–R&D relationship," *Econometrica* 52(5): 1219–1240.

Hausman, J. and D. McFadden (1984), "Specification tests for the multinomial logit model," *Econometrica* 52: 1219–1240.

Henderson, R.M. (1988), "The failure of established firms in the face of technical change: A study of photolithographic alignment equipment," Unpublished dissertation, Harvard University.

Hennart, J.F. and Y.R. Park (1993), "Greenfield vs. acquisition – the strategy of Japanese investors in the United States," *Management Science* 39(9): 1054–1070.

Hergert, M. and D. Morris (1988), "Trends in international collaborative agreements," in F. Contractor and P. Lorange (eds), *Cooperative Strategies in International Business*, Lexington, Mass.: Lexington Books.

Hill, C.W.L., M.A. Hitt, and R.E. Hoskisson (1992), "Cooperative vs. competitive structures in related and unrelated diversified firms," *Organization Science* 3(4): 501–521.

Hounshell, D.A. and J.K. Smith (1985), "Du Pont: Better things for better living through research," Paper presented at the Hagley Conference, Wilmington, Del.

Irvine, J. and B.R. Martin (1983), "Assessing basic research: Some partial indicators of scientific progress in radio astronomy," *Research Policy* 12(2): 61–90.

Jacquemin, A. and C.H. Berry (1979), "Entropy measure of diversification and corporate growth," *Journal of Industrial Economics* 27: 359–369.

Jaffe, A.B. (1985), "Quantifying the effects of technological opportunity and research spillovers in industrial innovation," Unpublished Ph.D. dissertation, Harvard University, Department of Economics.

Jaffe, A.B. (1986), "Technological opportunity and spillovers of R&D: evidence from firms' patents, profits, and market value," *American Economic Review* 76(3): 984–1001.

Jaffe, A.B. (1988), "Demand and supply influences in R&D intensity and productivity growth," *Review of Economics and Statistics* 70(3): 431–437.

Jaffe, A.B. (1989a), "Characterizing the 'technological position' of firms, with application to quantifying technological opportunity and research spillovers," *Research Policy* 18: 87–97.

Jaffe, A.B. (1989b), "Real effects of academic research," *American Economic Review* 79(5): 957–970.

Jaffe, A.B., M. Trajtenberg, and R.M. Henderson (1993), "Geographic localization of knowledge spillovers as evidenced by patent citations," *Quarterly Journal of Economics* 108(3): 577–598.

Jensen, M. (1986), "Agency costs of free cash flow, corporate finance, and takeovers," *American Economic Review* 76, May: 323–329.

Klein, B., R.A. Crawford, and A. Alchian (1978), "Vertical integration, appropriable rents, and the competitive contracting process," *Journal of Law and Economics* 21: 297–326.

Kogut, B. and D.J. Kim (1994), "Technological platforms and diversification," Unpublished manuscript, Wharton School, University of Pennsylvania.

Kogut, B. and H. Singh (1988), "The effect of national culture on the choice of entry mode," *Journal of International Business Studies* 19: 411–432.

Kortum, S. and J. Putnam (1989a), "Estimating patents by industry: Part 1," Unpublished manuscript, Yale University.

Kortum, S. and J. Putnam (1989b), "Estimating patents by industry: Part 2," Unpublished manuscript, Yale University.

Kreps, D. (1990), *Game Theory and Economic Modelling*, Oxford: Oxford University Press.

Kuznets, S. (1962), "Inventive activity: Problems of definition and measurement," in R.R. Nelson (ed.), *The Rate and Direction of Inventive Activity*, Princeton: Princeton University Press.

Lamont, B.T. and C.R. Anderson (1985), "Mode of corporate diversification and economic performance," *Academy of Management Journal* 28: 926–934.

Lecraw, D.J. (1984), "Diversification strategy and performance," *Journal of Industrial Economics* 13: 179–198.

Lemelin, A. (1982), "Relatedness in the patterns of interindustry diversification," *Review of Economics and Statistics* 64: 646–657.

Lev, B. and T. Sougiannis (1993), "The capitalization, amortization and value-relevance of R&D," *Working Paper BPP-56*, University of California, April.

Levin, R.C., W.M. Cohen, and D.C. Mowery (1985), "R-and-D appropriability, opportunity, and market structure – new evidence on some Schumpeterian hypotheses," *American Economic Review* 75: 20–24.

Levin, R.C., A.K. Klevorick, R.R. Nelson, and S.G. Winter (1987), "Appropriating the returns from industrial research and development," *Brookings Papers on Economic Activity* 3: 783–833.

Levin, R.C. and P.C. Reiss (1988), "Cost-reducing and demand-creating research-and-development with spillovers," *Rand Journal of Economics* 19(4): 538–556.

Levy, D.T. (1989), "Firm-specific assets and diversification," *Journal of Industrial Economics* 36(2): 227–233.

Li, J.T. (1994), "Foreign entry and survival: Effects of strategic choices on performance in international markets," *Strategic Management Journal* 16(5): 333–351.

Lippman, S. and R.P. Rumelt (1982), "Uncertain imitability: An analysis of interfirm differences in efficiency under competition," *Bell Journal of Economics* 13: 418–453.

Lubatkin, M. (1987), "Merger strategies and stockholder value," *Strategic Management Journal* 8: 39–53.

Lubatkin, M., H. Merchant, and N. Srinivasin (1993), "Construct validity of some unweighted product-count diversification measures," *Strategic Management Journal* 14(6): 433–449.

MacDonald, J.M. (1985), "R&D and the direction of diversification," *Review of Economics and Statistics* 67: 583–590.

Maddala, G.S. (1983), *Limited-Dependent and Qualitative Variables in Econometrics*, Cambridge: Cambridge University Press.

Mahoney, J.T. and J.R. Pandian (1992), "The resource-based view within the conversation of strategic management," *Strategic Management Journal* 13: 363–380.

Mansfield, E. (1984), "R&D and innovation: Some empirical findings," in Z. Griliches (ed.), *R&D, Patents and Productivity*, Chicago: University of Chicago Press.

Mansfield, E. (1986), "Patents and innovation: an empirical study," *Management Science* 32(2): 173–181.

Mansfield, E., M. Schwartz, and S. Wagner (1981), "Imitation costs and patents: An empirical study," *Economic Journal* 91: 907–918.

Manski, C.F. and D. McFadden (1981), "Alternative estimators and sample designs for discrete choice analysis," in C.F. Manski and D. McFadden (eds), *Structural Analysis of Discrete Data with Econometric Applications*, Cambridge: MIT Press.

Mitchell, W. (1992), "Are more good things better, or will technical and market capabilities conflict when a firm expands?" *Journal of Industrial and Corporate Change* 1: 327–346.

Montgomery, C.A. (1981), "The measurement of firm diversification: Some new empirical evidence," *Academy of Management Journal* 25: 299–307.

Montgomery, C.A. (1985), "Product-market diversification and market power, *Academy of Management Journal* 28: 789–798.

Montgomery, C.A. (1994), "Corporate diversification," *Journal of Economic Perspectives* 8(3): 163–178.

Montgomery, C.A. and S. Hariharan (1991), "Diversified expansion by large established firms," *Journal of Economics, Behavior and Organization* 15: 71–89.

Montgomery, C.A. and B. Wernerfelt (1988), "Diversification, Ricardian rents, and Tobin's q," *Rand Journal of Economics* 19: 623–632.

Mowery, D.C. (1983), "Industrial research and firm size, survival, and growth in American manufacturing, 1921–1946," *Journal of Economic History* 43: 953–980.

Narin, F., E. Noma, and R. Perry (1987), "Patents as indicators of corporate technological strength," *Research Policy* 16: 143–155.

National Science Board (1991), *Science and Engineering Indicators*, Washington, DC: US Government Printing Office.

Nayyar, P.R. (1993), "Stock market reactions to related diversification moves by service firms seeking information asymmetries and economies of scope," *Strategic Management Journal* 14(8): 569–591.

Nelson, R.R. and S.G. Winter (1982), *An Evolutionary Theory of Economic Change*, Cambridge: Harvard University Press.

Orr, D. (1974), "The determinants of entry: A study of the Canadian manufacturing industries," *Review of Economics and Statistics* 56: 58–66.

OTAF (Office of Technology Assessment and Forecast) (1985), "Review and assessment of the OTAF concordance between the US patent classification and the standard industrial classification systems: Final report," Unpublished manuscript.

Pakes, A. (1985), "On patents, R&D, and the stock market rate of return," *Journal of Political Economy* 93(2): 390–409.

Pakes, A. (1986), "Patents as options: Some estimates of the value of holding European patent stocks," *Econometrica* 54(4): 755–784.

Pakes, A. and Z. Griliches (1980), "Patents and R&D at the firm level: A first report," *Economic Letters* 5(4): 377–381.

Pakes, A. and Z. Griliches (1984), "Patents and R&D at the firm level: A first look," in Z. Griliches (ed.), *R&D, Patents, and Productivity*, Chicago: University of Chicago Press.

Pakes, A. and M. Schankerman (1984), "The rate of obsolescence of patents, research gestation lags, and the private rate of return to research resources," in Z. Griliches (ed.), *R&D, Patents and Productivity*, Chicago: University of Chicago Press.

Palepu, K. (1985), "Diversification strategy, profit performance and the entropy measure," *Strategic Management Journal* 6, July: 239–255.

Panzar, J. and R. Willig (1975), "Economies of scale and economics of scope in multioutput production," Unpublished working paper, Bell Labs, Murray Hill, N.J.

Patel, P. and K. Pavitt (1987), "Is Western Europe losing the technological race?" *Research Policy* 16: 59–85.

Patel, P. and K. Pavitt (1991), "Large firms in the production of the world's technology: An important case of 'non-globalization,'" *Journal of International Business Studies* 22: 1–21.

Patel, P. and K. Pavitt (1994), "Technological competencies in the world's largest firms: Characteristics, constraints and scope for managerial choice," Unpublished manuscript, Science Policy Research Unit, University of Sussex.

Pavitt, K. (1982), "R&D, patenting, and innovative activities," *Research Policy* 11: 33–51.

Pavitt, K. (1984), "Sectoral patterns of technical change: Towards a taxonomy and a theory," *Research Policy* 13: 343–373.

Pavitt, K. (1985), "Patent statistics as indicators of innovative activities: Possibilities and problems," *Scientometrics* 7(1–2): 77–99.

Pavitt, K. (1994), "The technological competencies of the world's largest firms," Paper presented at the Université de Québec a Montreal, 18 February.

Pavitt, K., M. Robson, and J. Townsend (1989), "Technological accumulation, diversification and organization of UK companies 1945–1983," *Management Science* 35, January: 1.

Pennings, J.M., H.G. Barkema, and S.W. Douma (1994), "Organizational learning and diversification," *Academy of Management Journal* 37(3): 608–640.

Penrose, E.T. (1952), "Biological analogies in the theory of the firm," *American Economic Review* 62(5): 814–815.

Penrose, E.T. (1953), "Biological analogies in the theory of the firm – a rejoinder," *American Economic Review* 63(4): 600–609.

Penrose, E.T. (1959), *The Theory of the Growth of the Firm*, New York: Wiley & Sons.

Peteraf, M.A. (1993), "The cornerstones of competitive advantage: A resource-based view," *Strategic Management Journal* 14(3): 179–191.

Pfeffer, J. and G.R. Salancik (1978), *The External Control of Organizations: A Resource Dependence Perspective*, New York: Harper & Row.

Pisano, G.P. (1988), "Innovation through markets, hierarchies, and joint ventures: technology strategy and collaborative arrangements in the biotechnology industry," Unpublished dissertation, Haas School of Business, UC Berkeley.

Pisano, G.P. (1990), "The R&D boundaries of the firm: An empirical analysis," *Administrative Science Quarterly* 35(1): 153–176.

Pitts, R.A. (1976), "Diversification strategies and organizational policies of large diversified firms," *Journal of Economics and Business* 28: 191–199.

Pitts, R.A. (1977), "Strategies and structures for diversification," *Academy of Management Journal* 20: 197–208.

Pitts, R.A. (1980), "Toward a contingency theory of multibusiness organization design," *Academy of Management Journal* 5: 203–210.

Polanyi, M. (1958), *Personal Knowledge: Towards a Post Critical Philosophy*, Chicago: University of Chicago Press.

Porter, M.E. (1980), *Competitive Strategy*, New York: Free Press.

Powell, W.W. (1990), "Neither market nor hierarchy: Network firms of organizations," in L.L. Cummings and B. Staw (eds), *Research in Organizational Behavior* 12: 295–336.

Prahalad, C.K. and G. Hamel (1990), "The core competence of the corporation," *Harvard Business Review* 68: 79–91.

Ramanujam, V. and P. Varadarajan (1989), "Research on corporate diversification: A synthesis," *Strategic Management Journal* 10: 523–551.

Ravenscraft, D.R. and F.M. Scherer (1987), *Mergers, Sell-offs and Economic Efficiency*, Washington, DC: Brookings Institution.

Reinganum, J. (1983), "Uncertain innovation and the persistence of monopoly," *American Economic Review* 73: 741–748.

Robins, J. and M. Wiersema (1995), "A resource-based approach to the multi-business firm: Empirical analysis of portfolio inter-relationships and corporate financial performance," *Strategic Management Journal* 16(4): 277–299.

Rumelt, R.P. (1974), *Strategy, Structure, and Economic Performance*, Cambridge: Harvard University Press.

Rumelt, R.P. (1982), "Diversification strategy and profitability," *Strategic Management Journal* 3: 359–369.

Salter, M.S. and W.S. Weinhold (1979), *Diversification Through Acquisition*, New York: Free Press.

Sanders, B. (1962), "Some difficulties in measuring inventive activity," in R.R. Nelson (ed.), *The Rate and Direction of Inventive Activity*, Princeton: Princeton University Press.

Sanders, B. (1964), "Patterns of commercial exploitation of patented inventions by large and small corporations," *Patent, Trademark, Copyright Journal of Research and Education* 8: 51–92.

Schankerman, M. and A. Pakes (1986), "Estimates of the value of patent rights in European countries during the post-1950 period," *Economic Journal* 96: 1052–1076.

Scherer, F.M. (1965), "Firm size, market structure, opportunity, and output of patented innovations," *American Economic Review* 55: 1097–1125.

Scherer, F.M. (1980), *Industrial Market Structure and Economic Performance*, Chicago: Rand-McNally.

Scherer, F.M. (1982a), "Demand-pull and technological innovation: Schmookler revisited," *Journal of Industrial Economics* 30(3): 225–237.

Scherer, F.M. (1982b), "The Office of Technology Assessment and Forecast industry concordance as a means of identifying industry technology origins," *World Patent Information* 4(1): 2–17.

Scherer, F.M. (1984a), "Using linked patent and R&D data to measure interindustry technology flows," in Z. Griliches (ed.), *R&D, Patents, and Productivity*, Chicago: University of Chicago Press.

Scherer, F.M. (1984b), "Interindustry technology flows and productivity growth," in F.M. Scherer (ed.), *Innovation and Growth: Schumpeterian Perspectives*, Cambridge: MIT Press.

Schmookler, J. (1962a), "Changes in industry and in the state of knowledge as determinants of industrial invention," in R.R. Nelson (ed.), *The Rate and Direction of Inventive Activity*, Princeton: Princeton University Press.

Schmookler, J. (1962b), "Comment [on Sanders and Kuznets]," in R.R. Nelson (ed.), *The Rate and Direction of Inventive Activity*, Princeton: Princeton University Press.

Schmookler, J. (1966), *Invention and Economic Growth*, Cambridge: Harvard University Press.

Schmookler, J. (1972), *Patents, Invention, and Economic Change* (Z. Griliches and L. Hurwicz, eds), Cambridge: Harvard University Press.

Schumpeter, J.A. ([1942] 1950), *Capitalism, Socialism and Democracy*, New York: Harper.

Scott, J.T. (1982), "Multimarket contact and economic performance," *Review of Economics and Statistics* 64, August: 368–375.

Scott, J.T. (1993), *Purposive Diversification and Economic Performance*, Cambridge: Cambridge University Press.

Scott, J.T. and G. Pascoe (1987), "Purposive diversification of R&D in manufacturing," *Journal of Industrial Economics* 36(2): 193–205.

Shen, T.Y. (1970), "Economies of scale, Penrose-effect, growth of plants and their size distribution," *Journal of Political Economy* 78: 702–716.

Shleifer, A. and R.W. Vishny (1991), "Takeovers in the '60s and the '80s: Evidence and implications," *Strategic Management Journal* 12, Winter: 51–59.

Simmonds, P.G. (1990), "The combined diversification breadth and mode dimensions and the performance of large diversified firms," *Strategic Management Journal* 11(5): 399–410.

Singh, H. and C. Montgomery (1987), "Corporate acquisition strategies and economic performance," *Strategic Management Journal* 8, July–August: 377–386.

Singh, H. and P.N. Subbanarasimha (1993), "The role of corporate technological knowledge in market entry, exit and performance," Paper presented at Academy of Management meeting, August 4, Atlanta.

Slater, M. (1980), "The managerial limitations to the growth of firms," *Economic Journal* 90: 520–528.

Soete, L. (1983), "Comments on the OTAF concordance between the US SIC and the US patent classification," Unpublished manuscript, Science Policy Research Unit, University of Sussex, November.

Statistics Canada (1990), *Concordance Between the Standard Industrial Classifications of Canada and the United States*, Ottawa: Statistics Canada.

Stewart, T. (1994), "Your company's most valuable asset: Intellectual capital," *Fortune*, October 3: 68–74.

Streitweiser, M. (1991), "The extent and nature of establishment-level diversification in 16 United States manufacturing industries," *Journal of Law and Economics* 34(2): 503–534.

Teece, D.J. (1977), "Technology transfer by multinational firms: The resource cost of international technology transfer," *Economic Journal* 87.

Teece, D.J. (1980), "Economics of scope and the scope of the enterprise," *Journal of Economic Behavior and Organization* 1: 223–247.

Teece, D.J. (1981), "The market for know-how and the efficient international transfer of technology," *Annals of the AAPSS* 458 (November): 81–96.

Teece, D.J. (1982), "Towards an economic theory of the multiproduct firm," *Journal of Economic Behavior and Organization* 3: 39–63.

Teece, D.J. (1984), "Economic analysis and the nature of the firm," *California Management Review* 25(3): 87–110.

Teece, D.J. (1986), "Profiting from technological innovation," *Research Policy* 15: 286–305.

Teece, D.J. (1988), "Technological change and the nature of the firm," in G. Dosi *et al.* (eds), *Technical Change and Economic Theory*, London: Pinter.

Teece, D.J., G.P. Pisano, and A. Shuen (1992), "Firm capabilities, resources, and the concept of corporate strategy," Unpublished working paper, University of California at Berkeley, Haas School of Business.

Teece, D.J., R.P. Rumelt, G. Dosi, and S.G. Winter (1994), "Understanding corporate coherence: Theory and evidence," *Journal of Economic Behavior and Organization* 23(1): 1–32.

Trajtenberg, M. (1990), "A penny for your quotes: Patent citations and the value of innovations," *Rand Journal of Economics* 21(1): 172–187.

US Federal Trade Commission (1973–1976), *Statistical Report: Annual Line of Business Report*, Washington, DC: US GPO.

US Office of Patent Classification Systems (1985), *Concordance, United States Patent Classification to International Patent Classification* (5th edn), Washington, DC: US GPO.

Voigt, C.W. (1993), "The Trinet large establishment data," unpublished draft manuscript, University of California at Los Angeles, Anderson Graduate School of Management.

Wernerfelt, B. (1984), "A resource-based view of the firm," *Strategic Management Journal* 5: 171–180.

Wernerfelt, B. and C.A. Montgomery (1988), "Tobin's q and the importance of focus in firm performance," *American Economic Review* 78, March: 246–250.

Who Owns Whom. North America (1981), London: Dun & Bradstreet, Ltd., Directories Division.

Williamson, O.E. (1964), *The Economics of Discretionary Behavior: Managerial Objectives in a Theory of the Firm*, Englewood Cliffs, N.J.: Prentice-Hall.

Williamson, O.E. (1975), *Markets and Hierarchies: Analysis and Antitrust Implications*, New York: Free Press.

Williamson, O.E. (1985), *Economic Institutions of Capitalism*, New York: Free Press.

Williamson, O.E. (1988), "The logic of economic organization," *Journal of Law, Economics, and Organization* 4: 65–93.

Williamson, O.E. (1991), "Comparative economic organization: The analysis of discrete structural alternatives," *Administrative Science Quarterly* 36: 269–296.

Woolridge, J.R. and C.C. Snow (1992), "Stock market reaction to strategic investment decisions," *Strategic Management Journal* 14(3): 163–177.

Wrigley, L. (1970), "Divisional autonomy and diversification," Unpublished dissertation, Graduate School of Business, Harvard University.

Yip, G.S. (1982), "Diversification entry: Internal development versus acquisition," *Strategic Management Journal* 3: 331–345.

Index